8·24·78

The Secular Meaning
of the Gospel

The Secular Meaning of the Gospel BASED ON

AN ANALYSIS OF ITS LANGUAGE

Paul M. van Buren

THE MACMILLAN COMPANY, NEW YORK

COLLIER-MACMILLAN LIMITED, LONDON

Fourth Printing 1966

Designed by Andrew Roberts

The Macmillan Company, New York
Collier-Macmillan Canada, Ltd., Toronto, Ontario

Library of Congress catalog card number: 63-15701

Printed in the United States of America

Acknowledgments

Grateful acknowledgment is hereby made for permission to quote from the following published works:

To Faber and Faber Ltd., London, and to Random House, Inc., New York, for "Friday's Child" © copyright 1958 by W. H. Auden, reprinted from *Homage to Clio* by W. H. Auden, by permission of Random House, Inc.

To The Westminster Press, Philadelphia, for permission to quote from *Christology of the New Testament* © SCM Press, Ltd., 1959, and to SCM Press, Ltd., London, for permission to use this material.

To W. Kohlhammer Verlag, Stuttgart, for permission to quote from *Jesus von Nazareth* by G. Bornkamm, published 1956.

To Cambridge University Press, London, for permission to quote from R. B. Braithwaite, "An Empiricist's View of Religious Belief," copyright 1955 by Cambridge University Press; also for permission to quote from C. E. Raven, *Apollinarianism*, 1923.

To J. S. Bezzant, St. John's College, Cambridge, for permission to quote from *Foundations*, edited by B. H. Streeter, London, Macmillan, 1912.

To J. C. B. Mohr, Tübingen, Germany, for permission to quote from Bultmann, "Das Christologische Bekenntnis des Oeckumenischen Rates," in *Glauben und Verstehen*, Vol. II, Tübingen, Mohr, 1952.

To Thomas Nelson and Sons, New York, for permission to quote from the *Revised Standard Version of the Holy Bible*, copyright 1946 and 1952 by the Division of Christian Education of the National Council of Churches.

To the University Press, Edinburgh, for permission to quote from Erich Frank, *The Role of History in Christian Thought*, cited by Bultmann in *History and Eschatology*, Edinburgh, University Press, 1957.

Acknowledgments v

To Chr. Kaiser Verlag, Munich, for permission to quote from Dietrich Bonhoeffer, *Widerstand und Ergebung*, Munich, Chr. Kaiser Verlag, 1951.

To The Macmillan Company, New York, for permission to quote from *New Essays in Philosophical Theology*, edited by A. Flew and A. MacIntyre, London, SCM, 1955, and to SCM Press, Ltd., for permission to use this material.

To Basil Blackwell & Mott Limited for permission to quote from L. Wittgenstein, *Philosophical Investigations*, Oxford, Blackwell, 1958.

To Alec R. Allenson, Inc., Naperville, Ill., for permission to quote from E. Schweizer, *Lordship and Discipleship*, Allenson's, Naperville, 1960, and to SCM Press, Ltd., for permission to use this material.

To Harper and Row, New York, for permission to quote from *Christ Without Myth* by Schubert M. Ogden, copyright by Harper and Row, Publishers, Incorporated.

To SCM Press Limited, London, for permission to quote from *Religious Language* and *Freedom and Immortality* by Ian Ramsey.

To Anne

Friday's Child

In memory of Dietrich Bonhoeffer, martyred
at Flossenburg, April 9th, 1945

He told us we were free to choose
But, children as we were, we thought—
'Paternal love will only use
    Force in the last resort

On those too bumptious to repent.'—
Accustomed to religious dread,
It never crossed our minds He meant
    Exactly what He said.

Perhaps He frowns, perhaps He grieves,
But it seems idle to discuss
If anger or compassion leaves
    The bigger bangs to us.

What reverence is rightly paid
To a Divinity so odd
He lets the Adam whom He made
    Perform the Acts of God?

It might be jolly if we felt
Awe at this Universal Man;
(When kings were local, people knelt)
    Some try to, but who can?

The self-observed observing Mind
We meet when we observe at all
Is not alarming or unkind
    But utterly banal.

Though instruments at Its command
Make wish and counterwish come true,
It clearly cannot understand
    What it can clearly do.

Since the analogies are rot
Our senses based belief upon,
We have no means of learning what
    Is really going on,

And must put up with having learned
All proofs or disproofs that we tender
Of His existence are returned
    Unopened to the sender.

Now, did He really break the seal
And rise again? We dare not say;
But conscious unbelievers feel
    Quite sure of Judgment Day.

Meanwhile, a silence on the cross,
As dead as we shall ever be,
Speaks of some total gain or loss,
    And you and I are free

To guess from the insulted face
Just what Appearances He saves
By suffering in a public place
    A death reserved for slaves.

— W . H . A U D E N

From *Homage to Clio*

PREFACE

What is the Gospel? What is secularism? An author who sets out to find the secular meaning of the Gospel might be expected to have these polar terms clearly in hand. We confess at once that we do not. We can suggest certain features that have been central in some interpretations of the Gospel, and we can suggest other features which seem to characterize secularism. Since we have no Archimedean point from which to make any final decisions about either question, we must accept the fact that we speak from within a period in which there is considerable confusion about the nature of both Christianity and secularism.

Taking secularism as a loose designation of the reaction to the Idealism of the last century, we may say that both modern so-called biblical theology and modern so-called analytic philosophy are responses to secularism. The strictly non-Archimedean point from which this book is written is that of one who detects and affirms something in common in each of these modern movements in theology and philosophy and also in himself. Call this common feature certain empirical attitudes. Call it a deep interest in questions of human life this side of the "beyond," and a corresponding lack of interest in what were once felt to be great metaphysical questions. Call it secularism. The question to which this book is addressed is a frankly autobiographical one and will have wider interest to the extent that others stand at or near the place from which it is asked. The question is: How may a Christian who is himself a secular man understand the Gospel in a secular way? In the exploration of this question, it is hoped that the meaning both of the Gospel and of secularism will become clearer, and that for some at least this clarity may help them to see more clearly the point at which they stand, regardless of its name.

This study has grown out of many conversations, oral and written, with many people. Beyond sources indicated in footnotes, I wish to acknowledge particularly the help, criticisms and encouragement I have received—without in any way implying their responsibility for what I have written—from Karl Barth, Ian T. Ramsey, Eduard Schweizer, Ruel W. Tyson, Hugh C. White, and E. R. Wickham, and especially from William A. Clebsch and William H. Poteat, who read the manuscript in its next-to-last stage and whose criticisms have been most helpful. I would especially acknowledge the labors of her to whom this book is dedicated, who helped at every stage of its development. I wish also to express my thanks to the Board of Trustees of the Episcopal Theological Seminary of the Southwest and to the American Association of Theological Schools for making available the time to write this book. I am indebted to Frederick L. Chenery for reading the proofs.

Scriptural quotations are from the Revised Standard Version of the Holy Bible copyrighted 1946 and 1952 by the Division of Christian Education of the National Council of Churches and used by permission.

PAUL M. VAN BUREN

CONTENTS

Part Two

I

INTRODUCTION

The Contemporary Problem for Theology and Faith: A Secular Understanding of the Gospel

"Honesty demands that we recognize that we must live in the world as if there were no God. And this is just what we do recognize—before God! God himself drives us to this realization. —God makes us know that we must live as men who can get along without Him. The God who is with us is the God who forsakes us (Mark 15:34)! We stand continually in the presence of the God who makes us live in the world without the God-hypothesis."[1]

With these words, Dietrich Bonhoeffer described his situation as a Christian in a world "come of age," in which men no longer, believe in a transcendent realm where their longings

[1] Dietrich Bonhoeffer, *Widerstand und Ergebung* (Munich: Chr. Kaiser Verlag, 1951), p. 241. English translation, *Letters and Papers from Prison* (London: SCM Press, 1953), pp. 163 f. Published in the U.S. under the title *Prisoner for God* (N.Y.: Macmillan, 1957). I have made my own translation. Hereafter referred to as *WE*. Corresponding page references in published translations will be in parentheses.

will be fulfilled. Wishing not to retreat from this new world, Bonhoeffer began what he called a "nonreligious interpretation of biblical concepts." He had scarcely the time to outline his proposal in a few letters written from prison before his death.

Bonhoeffer made his proposal as a theologian and as a believer. As a theologian, he asserted that it offered the only way to overcome weaknesses of the "liberal" theology inherited from the past century, without neglecting or refusing to answer the question it posed.[2] We take this to mean that he wanted to retrieve from the smothering arms of the religious subjectivity of "liberal" theology the concern of traditional theology for God's work in Jesus Christ, and yet to acknowledge the critical study of the biblical documents and traditional formulations of Christian faith undertaken in the nineteenth century. He was apparently also concerned as a believer to find an appropriate way for a Christian in a world "come of age" to confess his faith in Jesus Christ. He did not write as a professional Christian or qualified theologian who understood the Gospel perfectly clearly and was only looking for a technique of communication or popular idiom to reach the man of today "out there," outside the church. On the contrary, he wrote as a citizen of this modern, adult world, as much inclined as the next man to consult the weather map and the meteorologist for the answer to a question about a change in the weather, rather than to "take it to the Lord in prayer." Modern man is not "out there" to be spoken to; he is within the being of every Christian trying to understand. Bonhoeffer refused to retreat from his ordinary way of thinking into a Christian ghetto of traditional formulae in order to preserve his faith. His question still lies before us: How can the Christian who is himself a secular man understand his faith in a secular way? We intend to answer this question with the help of a method far removed from Bonhoeffer's thought. The answer will be reached by analyzing what a man

[2] *Ibid.*, p. 221 (149).

means when he uses the language of faith, when he repeats the earliest Christian confession: "Jesus is Lord."

Our proposal to answer Bonhoeffer's question by analyzing the language of faith has been suggested to us by the work of philosophers, of whom there are now many in the English-speaking world, who practice "linguistic analysis." Linguistic analysis is what this name implies: a method, not a philosophical doctrine. It simply clarifies the meaning of statements by investigating the way in which they are ordinarily used. The way in which this method exposes the problem of the language of faith for men today may be indicated by a parable told by Anthony Flew, a British philosopher.[3]

"Once upon a time two explorers came upon a clearing in the jungle. In the clearing were growing many flowers and many weeds. One explorer says, 'Some gardener must tend this plot.' The other disagrees. 'There is no gardener.' So they pitch their tents and set a watch. No gardener is ever seen. 'But perhaps he is an invisible gardener.' So they set up a barbed wire fence. They electrify it. They patrol with bloodhounds. . . . But no shrieks ever suggest that some intruder has received a shock. No movement of the wire ever betrays an invisible climber. The bloodhounds never give cry. Yet still the Believer is not convinced. 'But there is a gardener, invisible, intangible, insensible to electric shocks, a gardener who has no scent and makes no sound, a gardener who comes secretly to look after the garden which he loves.' At last the Sceptic despairs, 'But what is left of your original assertion? Just how does what you call an invisible, intangible, eternally elusive gardener differ from an imaginary gardener or even from no gardener at all?' " Flew concludes, "A fine brash hypothesis may thus be killed by inches, the death of a thousand qualifications."[4]

[3] Flew acknowledges that his parable is based on a story in John Wisdom's article "Gods," originally published in *Proceedings of the Aristotelian Society*, 1944, but available in Professor Wisdom's *Philosophy and Psychoanalysis* (Oxford: Blackwell, 1953), pp. 154 ff.

[4] *New Essays in Philosophical Theology*, A. Flew and A. MacIntyre, ed. (London: SCM Press, 1955), pp. 96 f. Hereafter referred to as *New Essays*.

Many believers will react to these words by searching at once for some hole in the argument or for some counterargument. It is wiser to resist this temptation long enough to hear the simple point and the straightforward question in the parable. The point is not unlike Bonhoeffer's. Whatever ancient man may have thought about the supernatural, few men are able today to ascribe "reality" to it as they would to the things, people, or relationships which matter to them. Our inherited language of the supernatural has indeed died "the death of a thousand qualifications." Flew's point is that the Believer has said no more than the Sceptic about "how things are." His implied question, then, is reasonable and straightforward: Can the Christian today give any account of his words? Can he say what he means, and does he mean what he says, when he repeats the ancient apostolic confession? The unbelieving philosopher has spoken more sharply than the believing theologian, but their questions are closely related. Taken together, they pose the central question for contemporary faith and theology.[5]

Since the end of the Second World War, Protestant theology has been occupied with the same question, but the question has been put in yet a different form, arising from the proposal of the New Testament scholar and theologian Rudolf Bultmann to "demythologize" the New Testament message and to interpret it in terms of the existentialist philosophy of Martin Heidegger.[6]

---

[5] The question of a proper way in which to speak of God, or indeed whether it is proper to speak of him at all, is hardly new. Anyone familiar with the thought of the Old Testament is aware of the special problem this question posed in this history of Hebrew and Jewish thought, and of the measures taken to avoid speaking the divine name "Yahweh." It might be argued that the problem to which this study is addressed has arisen from the fact that the Christian Church never adequately appreciated this reticence. Be that as it may, Bonhoeffer and especially Flew have nevertheless raised questions which are particularly those of our own time.

[6] Bultmann's original proposal was published in 1941. It forms the opening essay in the first volume of the series containing the main documents in the controversy: *Kerygma und Mythos,* H. Bartsch, ed. (Hamburg: Herbert Reich-Evangelischer Verlag, 1948), hereafter referred to as *Kerygma und Mythos.* The first volume has been translated by R. H. Fuller, *Kerygma and Myth* (New York: Harper, 1961). Bultmann has presented his proposal in a more discursive form in

This proposal focuses on modern man's inability to understand the mythological setting of the New Testament message and it presents an interpretation based on a particular analysis of human existence. Bultmann intends both to preserve the message of the New Testament and its historical foundation in the event of Jesus Christ and also to satisfy the needs of a contemporary understanding of that message; his double intention is related to the concerns of Bonhoeffer and Flew. Whether it meets Bonhoeffer's theological concern to overcome the limitations of nineteenth-century theology or the despair of the Sceptic over the meaninglessness of the language of the Believer in Flew's parable is another matter.

There are two sides to Bultmann's proposal. First, he is concerned about the incomprehensibility to contemporary man of the mythological form in which the kerygma, the apostolic proclamation, is expressed. Myth, as Bultmann uses the word, is the presentation of the transcendent in terms of this world. The New Testament is mythological in that it pictures the world as having three stories, with heaven above and the realm of the dead below. Divine action is conceived as an intervention in this world by heavenly, transcendent powers. But men today can no longer give credence to such a way of thinking. The scientific revolution, with its resulting technological and industrial developments, has given us another, empirical, way of thinking and of seeing the world. That which cannot be conceived in terms of man and the world explored by the natural sciences is simply without interest because it is not "real." For this reason, Bultmann feels that we have no alternative but to push further along the road opened in the nineteenth century, when the critique of ancient by modern thought was applied to the Bible and the documents of classical Christianity. We can no longer pretend that the Gospel can give information about "how things are" in the world. Bultmann is convinced, furthermore, that the New Testament authors themselves began the work of freeing .

his *Jesus Christ and Mythology* (New York: Scribner, 1958), which is a good introduction to the demythologizing controversy for non-theologians.

the kerygma from a mythological framework in order to present it in a way which touched the individual directly as a man where he was. In the Gospel of John, for example, the primitive proclamation of the breaking in of the Kingdom of God has become the proclamation of the gift of "eternal life," the word "eternal" suggesting a certain qualification of concrete human existence. Bultmann's conviction that the New Testament has already begun this process, and that the very nature of "faith," as the New Testament defines it, demands this sort of existentialist interpretation, supports him in his contention that the Gospel may and ought to be interpreted in a way which is not incompatible with the way men think today, which does not demand a *sacrificium intellectus* of contemporary believers.

The other side of Bultmann's proposal arises from his concern to put the kerygma, stripped of its mythological form and interpreted existentially, at the center of faith and theology. Faith is dependent upon the event of Jesus Christ, his appearance in history, his words and death. Although, according to Bultmann, an existentialist analysis of man can discover something of man's problem, and even define what an authentic existence would be, the kerygma alone offers man the possibility of this new existence, and the kerygma is grounded in the event of Christ. Bultmann has been attacked from the theological "right" for being too radical in interpreting the Gospel in existentialist terms, but he has also been criticized from the "left" for being too conservative, for compromising his existentialist interpretation by a refusal to dispense with a historical event of long ago as the basis of contemporary faith and authentic existence in the world today.

We agree with Bultmann that the kerygma expresses the heart of the Gospel, and we also agree that the whole tenor of thought of our world today makes the biblical and classical formulations of this Gospel unintelligible. Bultmann is accused of having failed to resolve this dilemma, but the alternatives offered by his critics to the right and to the left, arising from the discussion of his proposal, slight one or another aspect of the problem. The opening references to Bonhoeffer and especially to Flew suggest that there are other ways than Bultmann's to pose the contemporary question for faith and theology which may prove more fruitful to investigate.

The Two Sides of the Problem: Christology and Understanding

The criticisms of Bultmann's proposal from opposite positions reveal the two sides of the problem of a contemporary secular understanding of the Gospel. The objection coming from the right, represented by Karl Barth, is that Bultmann's existentialist interpretation of the kerygma throws out the baby with the bath water.[7] The whole of Barth's writing is a monument to the thesis that theologians should not concern themselves with the problem of the contemporary understanding of ancient thought, but should concentrate exclusively on the content of their discipline, which is the biblical testimony to God's self-revelation in Jesus Christ. The liberal theology of the nineteenth and early twentieth centuries came to a dead end, in Barth's judgment, precisely because it was dominated by an interest in man and his self-understanding, and he is convinced that the only way out of that impasse lies in returning to the proper concern of theology. The central doctrine for theology is Christology, not soteriology—the doctrine of the Saviour, not that of Salvation.

Understanding the Gospel, for Barth, comes only on the basis of faith, not apart from it;[8] from the point of view of faith

---

[7] Barth's objection to Bultmann's proposal may be found in his *Rudolf Bultmann, ein Versuch ihn zu Verstehen* (Zollikon-Zürich: Evangelischer Verlag, 1953). His own position is presented in his *Kirchliche Dogmatik* (Zollikon-Zürich: Evangelischer Verlag, 1952 f), referred to hereafter as *KD*, especially I/2, §§ 19-21, and IV/1, § 59. For Barth's Christology, cf. especially I/2, § 15 and IV/2, § 64. English translation, *Church Dogmatics*, ed. T. Torrance (Edinburgh: T. & T. Clark).

[8] Worked out in his study of Anselm, *Fides Quaerens Intellectum* (Munich: Chr. Kaiser, 1931), this thesis is the basis of Barth's order in *KD*, I/2, § 13: first the reality of revelation, and only then the discussion of its possibility. Cf. *KD*, I/1, § 6.

(and Barth will not allow that theology may take any other position seriously), there is no neutral ground from which one may even begin to understand the Gospel. Either one stands in faith *(fides qua creditur)* and seeks to understand what one believes *(fides quae creditur)*, or one stands outside faith and cannot understand the Gospel at all. We see light only by standing in the light. Barth feels that Bultmann, in beginning with the problem of understanding, has conformed faith to modern thought and distorted the Gospel. The "objective" side of the Gospel, God's act of grace in Jesus Christ, which took place before we were born and without our knowledge, seems to him to be in danger of being lost in the subjectivity of a new self-understanding.

For Barth, the kerygma announces an event, and if faith seeks understanding, it must begin by seeking to understand that event. The task of theology is to understand and interpret the biblical witness to Jesus of Nazareth, and this work is only done correctly when it is carried out in such a way as to be faithful to the apostolic proclamation. Because he understands the Fathers of the church as men who shared this exegetical concern, Barth, unlike Bultmann, has taken a sympathetic attitude toward patristic formulations of Christology and he has tried to understand the Fathers as one who joins them in their confession of Jesus Christ as very God and very man.[9] The fact that this confession may be literally nonsense to men today does not bother him. Nevertheless, this conservative alternative to Bultmann's proposal provides us with a fundamental principle for any restatement of the Gospel: Christian faith has to do with the New Testament witness to Jesus of Nazareth and what took place in his history. Christology, however it may be interpreted, will lie at the center of our understanding of the Gospel.

Barth has been in large part responsible for a rejuvenation of theology which has commanded serious attention even from

---

[9] This is granted by Roman Catholics. H. Volk, "Die Christologie bei Karl Barth und Emil Brunner," in *Das Konzil von Chalkedon,* III, (Würzburg: Echter, 1954), 618 ff.

Roman Catholic theologians. Bonhoeffer felt, however, that Barth had ignored the question of nineteenth-century theology.[10] Barth's criticism of Bultmann's proposal rests on the assumption that *what* we say may be considered without respect to *how* we say it. He ignores the fact that language functions in a historical context, that a man in twentieth-century America may repeat the words of a man in first-century Greece and yet use them in a different way, for a different purpose. Have these two hypothetical men said the same thing? Even if the Greek is translated into fully idiomatic English, is the meaning the same? Theological liberalism, whatever else may be said of it, at least took this problem seriously. It recognized that something has happened to our world and to ourselves in the past centuries which raises problems for our understanding of the language of man before the Renaissance. The radical teaching of Jesus or Paul about the Kingdom of God or the character of faith was not easily understood by their contemporaries. That problem remains, and we can thank Barth for insisting that it not be neglected. But another problem of understanding is at the root of the debate over demythologizing, and we should thank theological liberalism and Bultmann for reminding us of it.

Bultmann has been criticized not only from the "right" but also from the "left." While Barth fears that an existentialist interpretation of the Gospel threatens the Gospel itself, others charge that Bultmann's insistence on the kerygma and its historical foundation compromises his existentialist interpretation; it frustrates his intention to interpret the Gospel in a fully contemporary way. In binding faith to a particular incident in the distant past, he has retained a mythological element which violates "modern man's" self-understanding and leaves the Gospel as incomprehensible as before. This position, first expressed on the Continent by Fritz Buri,[11] has now found its advocate in the United States in Schubert M. Ogden, whose *Christ Without*

[10] *WE*, p. 221 (149).
[11] Buri's initial criticism is found in *Kerygma und Mythos*, II, 85-101.

Myth[12] presents, with careful documentation, the various sides of the debate over Bultmann's proposal, and we must acknowledge the convenience of his analysis of the controversy. He shows us that Bultmann's critics from both sides agree on the existence of a serious inconsistency in his proposal. Bultmann says, on the one hand, that faith must be interpreted exhaustively as the realization of man's original possibility of "authentic existence" as this is conceived by "an appropriate philosophical analysis." On the other hand, he insists that faith can only be realized because of the event of Jesus of Nazareth. Barth objects that the first thesis threatens the second; Ogden objects that the second negates the first.

Ogden's alternative includes Bultmann's existentialist interpretation of faith. According to him, the whole content of the Christian confession may be reduced to the assertion: "I henceforth understand myself no longer in terms of my past, but solely in terms of the future that is here and now disclosed to me in my encounter with the church's proclamation,"[13] so that "to believe" means to have this self-understanding, and to understand oneself in this way is to exist authentically. Because the Gospel addresses man as one who is without excuse (Rom. 2:1), he argues that man is responsible for his existence before, and apart from, being addressed by the Gospel. This responsibility is grounded in the fact that men are everywhere confronted by manifestations of God's love. If the Gospel were the only effective manifestation of that love, then it would have to say that from the time a man first hears it he is without excuse. Only a genuine possibility makes a man genuinely responsible. The Gospel, however, takes seriously the radical responsibility of man, which it could do only if authentic existence (or faith) were a universal human possibility. Authentic existence, therefore, cannot depend only on the event of Jesus of Nazareth. Even the apostolic conception of authentic existence may be discovered apart from the Gospel, in the existentialist philosophy of

12 Harper, New York, 1961.
13 Ogden, *op. cit.*, p. 114.

Heidegger. As Ogden reads the New Testament, the apostolic claim that God is revealed "only in Jesus Christ" means not that God can be found, or faith realized, only in him, but that the God made known in Jesus Christ is the only one there is: the God who is to be found everywhere. The logical conclusion would be that Christian faith is not dependent on the event of Jesus Christ. This conclusion is vitiated, however, by the fact that Ogden calls this event "the decisive manifestation" of "the unconditioned gift of God's love," which is the "ever-present ground and end of all created things."[14] Why the event of Jesus of Nazareth is "decisive" is not explained. If Bultmann is mistaken in saying that this event is "necessary" for faith, is Ogden not equally mistaken in calling it "decisive"? He should have said no more than that this event has proved helpful for some, but that others have arrived at the same goal by other means which they have found equally helpful.

Bultmann and Ogden are concerned about "modern man," the man who has never heard the Gospel, or who has rejected it as incomprehensible and unimportant. Their question is thus different from the one which introduces this study: "How can the Christian who is himself a secular man understand his faith in a secular way?" Bultmann and Ogden are asking how the Christian can preach the Gospel to secular modern man so that he will be able to hear, understand, and become a Christian. They are interested in the "modern man" who is outside the church. Our question has to do with the "modern man" who is inside the church, more or less, and who is wondering what he is doing there.

Bultmann and Ogden (unlike the theologians of the "right") acknowledge the problem to which Bonhoeffer and Flew each in his quite different way, have pointed. The mythological view of the world has gone, and with it went the possibility of speaking seriously of a *Heilsgeschichte:* a historical "drama of salvation," in which God is said to have acted at a certain time in this

[14] *Ibid.,* p. 153.

world to change the state of human affairs. The language of theologians is, moreover, as historically conditioned as that of other men. A theologian is more responsible to his subject matter if he admits this and gives some account of how he thinks and speaks. Bultmann has tried to do this by accepting the empirical, secular way in which we think normally. He has refused to conceive of faith as something beyond normal thought, and he has tried, therefore, to clarify the meaning of the Gospel in the terms of a contemporary mode of thought. His efforts, however, are marred by logical inconsistency.

The solution of the "left," represented by Ogden, has achieved consistency, however, at the cost of forfeiting the significant contribution to theology of the "right." Ogden says that Barth has taught us the importance of theological consistency, but Ogden has not taken as seriously (even though he mentions it) Barth's other lesson, that theology should be carried on in conversation with its own past.

The two alternatives to Bultmann are in a deadlock and they lead to mutually exclusive conclusions. More important, each alternative presents us with a choice we do not wish to make. The Christian is asked to exist today either by forfeiting the world in which he lives and his involvement in it, or by forgetting the historical basis of his faith and settling for a "Christ without myth," which turns out to be a Christ without Jesus. He is asked to abandon either his own historicity or that of the Gospel. Of course, this remark is an exaggeration: in fact, Barth goes a long way toward interpreting classical Christology in concepts less foreign to modern thought than those of the Fathers, and Ogden speaks of the significance of Jesus as a "definitive re-presentation of man's existence before God that has all the force of final revelation."[15] Both sides merit closer examination. The conflict, however, arises in part from the way in which both sides state the issue, of which Bultmann's famous dilemma is an example: "Does he [Jesus] help me because he is the Son of God,

---

[15] *Ibid.*, p. 161.

or is he the Son of God because he helps me?"[16] The temptation is to jump in on one side or the other, thereby accepting the form of the question as valid and clear. There would be more hope of moving ahead with the problem, however, if we began by analyzing the question itself. If we did, we might conclude with Ludwig Wittgenstein: "Say what you choose, so long as it does not prevent you from seeing the facts [of how we use language]. (And when you see them there is a good deal that you will not say.)"[17]

The Method and Nature of This Study

This remark of Ludwig Wittgenstein brings us back to Flew's parable, for Wittgenstein was one of the leaders in the development of linguistic analysis. Linguistic analysis may provide us with a useful tool for working on the contemporary problem of theology. The controversy over demythologizing has taken place mainly within the context of German theology. If English-speaking Christians are to make anything of the discussion for themselves, they may prefer to set up the problem in their own way. One English philosopher suggested that whereas Continental thought (Descartes, Spinoza, Kant and his Idealist successors) has tended traditionally to see man as spirit, mind, or mind linked with matter or nature, British thought has tended to have a less metaphysical, more historical understanding of man. Man has not been understood as mind in solidarity with infinite mind; man is seen simply as man and his solidarity is with men, a solidarity in history.[18] The thinking of the English-speaking world is also influenced by the tradition of British

---

[16] Bultmann, "Das christologische Bekenntnis des Oekumenischen Rates," in his Glauben und Verstehen (Tübingen: Mohr, 1952), II, 252. English translation by J. C. G. Greig, Essays Philosophical and Theological (London: SCM Press, 1955), p. 280.

[17] L. Wittgenstein, Philosophical Investigations (Oxford: Blackwell, 1953), § 79.

[18] M. B. Foster, in Faith and Logic, B. Mitchell, ed. (London: Allen & Unwin, 1957), p. 214.

empiricism, and this tendency is accentuated by the extent to which our culture is shaped by technology and industrialization. A philosophical method which shares this orientation reflects and enlightens the way in which we think and speak in daily life, and Christians of an industrialized society would do well to listen to it if they wish to take seriously the problem of how "modern man" thinks.

Linguistic analysis, although it is related historically to the Logical Positivism of the Vienna Circle of the 1920's, should not be confused with the somewhat dogmatic spirit and teachings of that philosophy.[19] Indeed, its deepest roots lie in the tradition of British empiricism. It is more accurate to speak of linguistic analysis as a method than a school or movement of philosophy, for what its practitioners share is only a common interest and a common logical method. Their interest is in the function of language, and their method lies in the logical analysis of how words and statements function, both in normal and in abnormal use. Linguistic analysts are not opposed in principle to the use of religious or theological language, as the logical positivists were. Indeed, some of them have produced interesting studies of religious and theological statements in the last ten years or so. Their work may be a significant contribution to the solution of the problem which has occupied theologians in the demythologizing controversy.

Logical Positivism judged all theological statements to be meaningless because they could not meet the verification principle of that philosophy: that, apart from the assertions of logic and mathematics, only those statements which can be verified or falsified empirically are meaningful statements. Statements having to do with an invisible, ineffable God, a transcendent "absolute," and the whole field of classical metaphysics in general could be neither proved nor disproved. Having no empirical

---

[19] For the following, cf. *Faith and Logic*, pp. 1 ff.; I. T. Ramsey, *Religious Language* (London: SCM Press, 1957), pp. 11-14; T. R. Miles, *Religion and the Scientific Outlook* (London: Allen & Unwin, 1959), pp. 16, 18 ff.

function, they could not be called true or false, and they were consequently regarded as meaningless. During the past quarter of a century, however, there has been a shift toward a more flexible conception of language. The verification principle has continued to be important, but it has another function in contemporary linguistic analysis. There are a variety of "language-games," activities with their appropriate languages,[20] and a modified verification principle is now used to ask what sort of things would count for an assertion and what sort of things would count against it. If we know that, we can say in which "language-game" the assertion is "at home." It is now recognized that different kinds of language are appropriate to different situations. The language of love is not that of biology, nor is the language of politics that of physics. The word "cause," for example, has different functions in the disciplines of physics, economics, and history. There is no reason why one should look for the same sort of evidence for a biologist's statement concerning a certain experiment and a statement of love by a lover. The modified verification principle can help us to sort out the pieces of our language, lest we try to understand the language of love in terms of biology or the language of politics in terms of physics.

This way of doing philosophy challenges the Christian to think clearly, speak simply, and say what he means without using words in unusual ways, unless he makes it quite clear what he is doing. A sentence from Ogden's book illustrates the appropriateness of this challenge: "When we say, then, that the integral significance of the event of Jesus is to re-present as a possibility demanding decision the final truth about man's existence *coram deo*, we are actually saying the reality this truth seeks to express is literally present 'in, with, and under' that

---

[20] The expression "language-game" is to be taken seriously. A trial for murder would be one sort of language-game, collective bargaining in industry would be another. "The *speaking* of language is part of an activity, or of a form of life." Wittgenstein, *op. cit.*, § 23; cf. § 7. On the variety of language-games, cf. §§ 65 ff.

same event." This, according to Ogden, is based on the "rule" that the "reality itself is actually present 'in, with, and under' the statement that seeks to express it."[21] Now this is clearly no general "rule." Applied to the statements of mathematics, it is nonsense. Applied to physics it is simply wrong. Applied to human relationships, it is puzzling. One wonders what Ogden is "actually saying." The purpose of linguistic analysis is to rid us of such cases of language cramps, when we cannot say just what we mean (and have to keep adding other sentences to say what we "actually" mean) and do not seem to mean just what we say.[22]

The question of *meaning,* under the title of "hermeneutics," has played an important part in Bultmann's program and in the ensuing discussion. Linguistic analysts have also considered this question; in fact, it has been central in their method, for an answer to the question of meaning is implied in the modified form of the verification principle. According to linguistic analysts, if we wish to know the meaning of a word or statement, we must look at the way it functions in actual use. The meaning of a word is not some invisible presence behind the word, some "ghost in the machine" (to use Gilbert Ryle's phrase). The meaning of a word is identical with its use.[23] We shall apply this deceptively simple, but (as we shall see) far-reaching, thesis of the linguistic analysts to the problem of a contemporary understanding of the Gospel, and it will clarify and help to dissolve some of the apparently insoluble conflicts which mark the current discussion in theology. Such questions as whether Jesus helps us because he is the Son of God or is the Son of God because he helps us, whether the Easter event is to be called "objective" or "subjective," and whether faith is or is not based

---

[21] Ogden, *op. cit.,* p. 161.

[22] It is evident that we do not agree with the somewhat superficial dismissal of linguistic analysis by C. Michalson, "The Ghost of Logical Positivism," in *The Christian Scholar,* XLIII/3, 1960, pp. 223 ff. In the same issue, compare the sensitive appreciation of Wittgenstein by John E. Smith, "The Impact of Wittgenstein," pp. 239 ff.

[23] "The meaning of a word is its use in the language." Wittgenstein, *op. cit.,* §43. This thesis and its supporting argument (§§ 1-42) is fundamental to our whole study.

on history, are in the center of contemporary theological discussion. We shall deal with them as Wittgenstein said one must deal with the problems of philosophy: "These are, of course, not empirical problems; they are solved, rather, by looking into the workings of our language, and that in such a way as to make us recognize those workings: *in despite of* an urge to misunderstand them. The problems are solved, not by giving new information, but by arranging what we have always known. Philosophy is a battle against the bewitchment of our intelligence by means of language."[24]

In turning to the method of linguistic analysis for assistance in finding the *meaning* of the Gospel, we shall be taking a somewhat different tack from most of those who have worked on the problem of Christian faith in a world "come of age." We do not reject the insights which existentialism has contributed, but we cannot forget that our English-speaking culture has an empirical tradition and that the world today is increasingly being formed by technology and the whole industrial process. Whether this is to be regretted or applauded, it is nevertheless the case. The language of existentialist theologians seems strange to the man whose job, community, and daily life are set in the context of the pragmatic and empirical thinking of industry and science, except perhaps in moments of exceptional personal crisis. In his daily life, the thinking of such a man—and we are all more or less this man—reflects the culture in which he lives. He thinks empirically and pragmatically.

A basic decision must be made by anyone who feels himself claimed by the Christian Gospel. Either "being a Christian" is something "religious" and quite distinct from secular affairs, or Christian faith is a human posture conceivable for a man who is part of his secular culture. What a Christian thinks about a given situation, the conclusions to which he comes, and the actions which he performs, may differ from those of one who is not a Christian. Whether they always will do so remains to be seen.

[24] *Ibid.*, § 109.

The question is whether a Christian is to be distinguished from an "unbeliever" by a different logic or thinking. Bonhoeffer contended that to separate Christian faith and secular life in the world is to reject the very heart of the Gospel, and we shall conduct this study on the assumption that "being a Christian" does not deny one's involvement in the secular world and its way of thinking. This assumption will govern our attempt to understand the Christian conviction that "Jesus is Lord." With the philosophical method of linguistic analysis already reflecting so clearly the way in which we think, speak, and understand today, it seems promising to try it as an interpretative tool. We have fundamentally nothing more to suggest than a certain "arrangement," as Wittgenstein put it, of what is already known, but it is our hope that by a fresh juxtaposition of the various elements of the problem, we shall suggest a fruitful line of development and contribute to the accomplishment of the theological task for our time.

Our task will be to describe and arrange three pieces of this puzzle: the conservative concern for Christology, the "liberal" concern with a contemporary way of thinking, and the logical analysis of theological statements. An examination of the christological emphasis of theologians of the "right" will show their faithfulness to the central concern of the theological tradition, and this will be illustrated by presenting an interpretation of Christology exemplifying the contemporary tendency to reconsider the patristic problem in the light of the insights of so-called biblical theology.[25] Such a Christology, however, although informed by recent research and contemporary ideas of man and history, will hardly escape the charge of being mythological, and it may be asked whether it is a contemporary interpretation at

---

[25] Although I believe this interpretation, which will be developed in the last section of Chapter II, to be my own, it will reveal the influence of Karl Barth, and parallels to various parts of it can be found in the writings of H. Diem, C. Welch, P. Althaus, G. Gogarten, C. Raven, G. von Rad and Ed. Schweizer. It is to that extent "typical." It represents my own position before I read Wittgenstein's *Philosophical Investigations*, and was suggested in my article "The Trinitarian Controversy Revisited," in *Religion in Life*, XXX (1960–61), 71-80.

all. Indeed, this is just the question of those who are concerned about the inability of modern man to understand the mythological form of the conservative interpretation. It must be asked, however, whether the position of the theological "left" has accepted the full implications of secularism, and whether it has done justice to theology's traditional concern with Jesus of Nazareth. These questions can be clarified with the help of studies of the nature of theological statements and the language of faith made by linguistic analysts, but the studies so far available on theological language do not, as they stand, quite fit the problem which confronts us.

A certain "arrangement" may help dissolve some of the dilemmas which beset contemporary theology, and it will also suggest a method for the constructive task which remains: to develop the consequences of this arrangement and the resulting method in sufficient detail to make clear their possibilities and limitations. As a point of departure, the relationship between the Gospel and the life, words, and death of Jesus is a matter that calls for careful linguistic analysis. This is a "historical" problem, dealing with a "historical" Gospel and a "historical" Jesus, and the question arises as to the meaning of the words "history" and "historical." Only by dealing with this question can one distinguish between sensible and nonsensical statements about Jesus as a figure in history and about the significance of what has been called "the Easter event" for the development of the Gospel in its various New Testament expressions and in the later language of theology. A careful, functional analysis of the language of the New Testament, the Fathers, and contemporary believers will reveal the secular meaning of the Gospel.

Before beginning our study, a preliminary remark is in order concerning our use of the word "secular." It may be said that this word has been used already in such a way as to imply some as yet undeclared commitments. We admit this implication. Just as Bonhoeffer's term "come of age" is a distinctly kerygmatic description of the modern world, so our use of "secular" as a designation of the modern world and modern thought is a function of the interpretation of the Gospel which this study will present. In a way, therefore, the word "secular" is redundant in the title of this study, but the way in which this is so will only become clear from the investigation itself.

When the world is called secular, the meaning of this word varies with the commitments of the speaker. Whether the speaker is a self-confessing "secularist" who means to distinguish himself from all "believers," or a "believer" using the word pejoratively, or, as in this study, a "believer" using the word positively, he is reflecting his commitments. None of these speakers, least of all the author, may claim to have found a neutral ground from which to describe "the way things are."

The modern revolt against Idealism is loosely what we have in mind when we speak of secularism, and the modern movements in theology and philosophy, roughly identified as kerygmatic theology and analytic philosophy, may be seen as responses to this revolt. A juxtaposition of these two movements and secularism, therefore, says something about the position from which this study is being made, as it sheds some light on what we are looking for when we ask after the secular meaning of the Gospel.

If we assume that secularism involves some grounding in empirical attitudes, it does not follow that secularism constitutes some neutral common ground of contemporary understanding. The "secular" world is not of one mind or even at all clear about the way its thought is or should be grounded empirically. To develop an interpretation of the Gospel on the basis of certain empirical attitudes, therefore, hardly serves an apologetic interest in making the Gospel understandable or more available to contemporary "unbelievers." It can only serve the purpose of faith seeking understanding. If other "believers" find that they too are struck by and committed to that which the author finds compelling in "secularism," they may also find this study helpful in seeking understanding. As the starting point of Part One will make clear, this book is a conversation "from faith to faith."

Part One

II

THE CONCERN

FOR CHRISTOLOGY

The Way to Chalcedon

A long and difficult way led from the first preaching of the kerygma to the formulation of the christological confession of the Council of Chalcedon in 451 A.D.[1] Since a survey of that whole route would take us far beyond our purposes here, we shall limit ourselves to a review of the forks in the road at which choices were made that were decisive for the future. It is a parody of the struggles and debates of those four centuries to present them as the continuous and unbroken development of the dogma defined at Chalcedon.[2] Such a conception betrays a

[1] A. Grillmeier's essay, "Die theologische und sprachliche Vorbereitung der christologischen Formel von Chalkedon," in Grillmeier and H. Bacht, eds., *Das Konzil von Chalkedon*, Vol. I (Würzburg: Echter Verlag, 1951), pp. 5-202; A. Gilg, *Weg und Bedeutung der altkirchlichen Christologie* (Munich: Chr. Kaiser Verlag, 1955); H. F. von Campenhausen, *Griechische Kirchenväter* (Stuttgart: W. Kolhammer, 1955), translated by Stanley Godman, *The Fathers of the Greek Church* (New York: Pantheon, 1959); C. E. Raven, *Apollinarianism* (Cambridge: Cambridge University Press, 1923); and A. von Harnack, *Lehrbuch der Dogmengeschichte*, have been my principal aids in the following summary and in interpreting the patristic material. Many of the important texts are available in good translation in *The Library of Christian Classics*, Vols. I, III, IV (Philadelphia: Westminster Press, 1953-54).

[2] H. von Campenhausen calls this "the fiction of an unbroken uniformity." *Op. cit.*, p. 167.

historical determinism ill fitted to the evidence, which can even lead to reading back into the past positions established at a later time. Attempts to find the doctrine of the incarnation of the second *persona* of the Trinity, or that of the two "natures" of Christ, in the New Testament, for example, are simply unhistorical reconstructions. To give another example, it is clear that Athanasius, in his essay on the Incarnation, simply did not consider the question (which became so important later) whether Jesus had a human soul. Strictly speaking, it would be more accurate to say that, by the standard of each conciliar definition, all earlier theology may be judged to be at least heterodox, for each new decision was made because earlier formulations had proved to be inadequate. The definition of "orthodoxy" was as open then as it is now, and it was altered not only by conciliar decisions but also by the predominance of one theological tendency or another. It is best, therefore, to understand how the formula of Chalcedon was realized, without using the labels "orthodox" or "heretic." It was only long after Chalcedon, moreover, that the Church could agree on what had actually been settled by that Council, and even then agreement was reached only at the cost of a major schism.

A choice was made at the beginning of the evolution of christological thought which was decisive for the future: the choice to understand Jesus as the incarnate Logos. This choice is already clearly expressed in the writings of Justin Martyr in the second century.[3] Justin, familiar with the stoic conception of the Logos as the all-pervasive rational principle of the universe, wrote not as an inventor but as a defender of the established conviction that this rational principle had taken on a human body, soul, and spirit. Prior to this Logos Christology, there had apparently been a Spirit Christology,[4] according to which Jesus had been a man possessed of the Spirit of God.

---

[3] For the following see especially E. R. Goodenough, *The Theology of Justin Martyr* (Jena: Frommannsche Buchhandlung Verlag, 1923).

[4] Grillmeier, *op. cit.*, pp. 9, 28; Gilg, *op. cit.*, pp. 17 ff.

However, by the middle of the second century it had given way in most places to an interpretation centering on the Logos. This idea was fruitful for the spread of Christianity in the Hellenistic world and helpful in defending the early Christians from the charge of worshiping a man. When they were charged with blasphemy for worshiping Jesus, they answered that their Lord Jesus Christ was not merely a man, but the eternal and universal Logos of God from which all order and rationality was derived. We should note some of the elements of which this Logos Christology was composed. This world, the realm of men, was thought to be a realm of corruption ruled by death. There was said to have been an incursion into it from the realm of the divine which had broken the grip of death. Death had been met and accepted by the enfleshed Logos and overcome on Easter; a way had thereby been opened for mankind and the whole of creation to enter the realm of incorruptibility. The framework of this thought was clearly what we have learned from Bultmann to call mythological, but however strange it may sound to us, we should remember that it contained good news for men in the second century who shared this picture of the structure of the universe and the plight of man.

Justin insisted that Jesus was a man like ourselves. Yet, as the man in whom the God-Logos was incarnate, he was distinct from all other men. By virtue of the special circumstances of his conception and birth, he had no historical relationship with the human race as other men have. By the act of the Logos, there was brought into the midst of the human race this one man who was like us, but whose origin set him quite apart from us. He possessed all the parts which make up a human being—body, soul, and spirit—yet it was right to call him Lord and to worship him, for this man was the Logos of God. This was the conception of Jesus which came to the minds of Christians in the second century when they read John 1:14, "The *Logos* became flesh and dwelt among us."

The assimilation of the idea of the Logos into Christian

doctrine was christological, not just theological. The Logos idea was not first used to solve a problem about God and his relationship to the world, but to justify the worship of Jesus of Nazareth. To be sure, Christians held, in common with their contemporaries, the idea of God as a rational, supreme, and unchangeable being, and the problem of the relationship of such a God to the world could be solved after a fashion by the interposition of the Logos, but the first and more urgent problem was a christological one: it was the question of the validity of their worship of the man Jesus of Nazareth.[5] Logos Christology was their answer to this problem.

The road to Chalcedon took a turn, however, when the Alexandrian thinkers—especially Origen—began to conceive of the Logos as almost equal to God. This development, coupled with a decision made in the middle of the third century, had far-reaching consequences. Christians were scattered about the ancient world in the third century, and a considerable variety of christological ideas could develop. Alexandria was the center of one line of thought, but another Christology was developed in Syria. It came to light in the teaching of Paul of Samosata, whose ideas became the subject of debate in Antioch and were condemned by a synod held there in 268 A.D. The roots of Paul's teaching lay in the early Spirit Christology: the understanding of Jesus as a man, born in a special way by God's decree, who, being ever more indwelt by the Spirit of God, became the perfect man and was consequently adopted as God's Son. This doctrine reflects a strong interest in Jesus himself—in his history as a real man—and this interest has made the ideas of Paul of Samosata attractive to some theologians in modern times.

The actual teaching of Paul can only be found in the outraged and sometimes vindictive writings of his opponents, but it seems from these fragments that he understood Jesus as a man whose will was so conformed to the will of God that finally he

[5] Goodenough, *op. cit.*, pp. 139 ff., 232 ff. For the contrary, see C. Richardson, *The Doctrine of the Trinity* (Nashville: Abingdon Press, 1958), pp. 56 ff.

became one with God, united in willing the same object. This teaching was condemned, apparently, because it was felt that it did not express adequately the unity between Jesus and God, or, more specifically, between Jesus and the divine Logos. To emphasize their point, the bishops of the Synod of Antioch maintained that the very essence of the Logos was incarnate in Jesus, which was not the case with other men. The difference between Jesus and all other men was defined as one of kind and not just one of degree.

The scene was thus prepared for a new definition of the problem. The Gospels said that Jesus died on the cross, and no one questioned the common idea of the impassibility of God: that the divine was by definition incapable of suffering any change. With the new conclusions, that the Logos was in the closest possible relationship to God, approaching identity (the tendency of Alexandrian teaching), and that Jesus was in the closest possible relationship to the Logos, which dwelt in him essentially (the conclusion of the Synod of Antioch), the simple Christology of Justin Martyr broke down. The following alternatives seemed possible:

First, one could deny the historical accuracy of the reports of the death of Jesus and say that an exchange had been made, so that it was not Jesus but someone else who had died on the cross; or (putting the idea in a more mythological form) that Jesus did not actually die, but only appeared to, and was received into heaven without passing by the way of suffering and death. The essential incarnation of the Logos in Jesus could thus be preserved without denying the identification of the Logos with God or the impassibility of the divine Logos. Although such a flagrant disregard of the sacred texts could not prevail, this alternative suggests the tendency of Alexandrian theology to qualify the concrete historicity of the man Jesus, and to conceive of his manhood in such a way that it remained untouched by the suffering and death which is the lot of all other men.

Second, a distinction could be made between the man Jesus who suffered and died and the divine Logos, so that it could be said that the man suffered while the Logos remained impassible. This distinction would tend to deny the unity of the incarnate Logos, a tendency of which the later Antiochene theologians and others associated with them were accused.

Finally, a distinction could be made between the Logos incarnate in the suffering Jesus and God, so that it could be said that the Logos suffered while God remained impassible. In this way, the biblical evidence of Jesus' death, the unqualified incarnation of the Logos in him, and the impassibility of God could all be preserved. The logical consequence of this idea, of course, would be that the Logos could not quite be God. This conclusion was made by Arius, whose position has been put in the form of a syllogism:[6] Christ was the incarnate Logos; Christ was subject to change; therefore, the Logos was subject to change. Granting the impassibility of God, the Logos could not be identified with him.

In order to preserve both the fact of the cross and the idea of God's impassibility, the idea of incarnation had to be qualified by drawing a line between God and the cross. Arius' solution was logical, but his decision to draw the line between God and the Logos undermined the earlier defense against the charge of worshiping a man rather than God. Fundamentally, this solution implied that what was seen in Jesus was something less than God; God himself might be other than that which was revealed in Jesus, perhaps a God of wrath rather than love. So serious a threat to the New Testament witness could not go unchallenged, and, regardless of the Arian logic the Council of Nicaea in 325 A.D. insisted that the Logos or Son of God was of one essence with the Father.

The eventual triumph of the Nicene definition eliminated the third possibility, but it left unsettled the choice between the

---

[6] Raven, *op. cit.,* p. 88.

other two. The line between God and the cross had still to be defined. Popular piety, especially in Egypt, tended to the first alternative, minimizing the suffering and the concrete historicity of Jesus. The incarnate Logos was understood as just that: the divine Logos in flesh, bearing a human body which it allowed to die while it was itself unmoved and passionless and omnipotent. The other tendency, which had appeared in the teaching of Paul of Samosata, was stronger in Syria, where a tradition of literal interpretation of the Bible was established, especially in Antioch. In that region, Christians insisted on the real sufferings of Jesus and his real death, and this emphasis made them draw the line between the suffering man and the impassible Logos. By the middle of the fourth century, the question of the relationship between God and man in Jesus Christ was as unsettled as it had ever been. The positions covered the range between two general types of Christology:[7] a Logos-flesh type, which arose in Egypt out of the defeat of Arianism, and a Logos-man type, centering in Antioch, in which the reality of Jesus as a man, who grew, developed, hungered, suffered, and died, was kept in view, even though this seemed to some to split Christ into a human Jesus and a divine Logos.

The final stage of the road to Chalcedon began with a reaction to the teaching of Apollinaris, bishop of Laodicea, which was condemned in 362 A.D. This was an extreme form of the Logos-flesh type of Christology, which carried the Alexandrian tendency to its logical conclusion. In the Incarnation, the Logos took on a human body vitalized by a human soul, which Apollinaris conceived as the animating principle of the body. According to Apollinaris, man is made up not only of a body and its animating principle, but also of *nous,* the rational principle of man. In Jesus, however, the human *nous* was replaced by the divine Logos. With this Christology, Apollinaris was able to confess one single Christ, a mixture of God and man, truly the

[7] Grillmeier, *op. cit.,* pp. 67 ff. and 124 ff.

God-man of earlier "orthodoxy," who suffered in his human aspect and triumphed over death by the power of his divine aspect. Christ was truly God (countering the Arian alternative), and yet not divided into two (countering the Antiochene tendency).

In the reaction to this teaching, there arose a new awareness of the significance of the historical side of Christology. How could God have come to terms with the human problem in Jesus, if Jesus were not a real man? The apostolic picture of Jesus as a man with a will and mind was replaced by one of an animated body without a human *nous*. Apollinaris' teaching was rejected, therefore, even if it only made explicit the implicit consequences of the traditional Logos-flesh Christology.

The last stage of the way to Chalcedon was marked by the struggle between the advocates of the two basic types. Cyril of Alexandria, the final leader of the old Egyptian tendency, stressed the unity of Christ at some cost to the reality of his manhood, and the theologians of the Antiochene tendency stressed the reality of Christ's manhood as well as of his divinity, at some cost to the unity of his being. The compromise which was agreed upon at the Council of Chalcedon, and which prevailed after long hesitation and many reconsiderations in the following centuries, combined the affirmations of both tendencies. This compromise was prepared for by a development of the terms "nature" and "person" or (to use the original word and to avoid confusion caused by our very different use of the word "person") *hypostasis*.

At first, "nature" and *hypostasis* were used synonymously, but they came to be distinguished with time, and this increase in technical terms made a compromise formula possible. When Christ was said to have two "natures," one divine and one human, this meant that he had that which marks a man as a man and distinguishes him from animals and angels, and that he had also that which marks the divine, in distinction from all creatures. Nothing that marks a man as a man was lacking to him, and also nothing that marks God as God. These two "natures" were united "inseparably, indivisibly, unchanged, and unconfused," according to the formula of Chalcedon, in one hypostasis, specifically in the hypostasis of the Logos. According to the implicit distinction of these terms, made explicit in the sixth century, the "nature" of anything is that which marks it for what it is, but its actual existence, that which allows it to be at all, is its hypostasis. Everything that is has a hypostasis and a "nature."

The final patristic answer to the christological problem was that the hypostasis of the Logos, having already a divine "nature," took on a human "nature" also. This human "nature" did not exist prior to or apart from this assumption (it was anhypostatic);[8] it began to be in the moment of being assumed by the hypostasis of the Logos (it was enhypostatic). The manhood of Jesus Christ, therefore, was considered to be constituted of a human "nature" and the hypostasis of the Logos. Freely translated, the late patristic christological answer asserted that Jesus was indeed a man as we are men, but the fact that he existed as a man was totally dependent on the fact that God the Word, the eternal Logos, had called him into being to be the historical bearer of this divine Word.

The conclusion of Chalcedon was refined by Leontius of Byzantium and given its classic expression in the writings of John of Damascus;[9] in this form it represents an attempt to gather together the threads of the two christological tendencies. The mystery of the Incarnation was preserved from dissolution by the doctrine of the hypostatic union: the union of the divine and human "natures" in the one hypostasis of the Logos. The

[8] Because of a mistranslation of hypostasis and anhypostasis, D. M. Baillie and others have spread the idea that this doctrine taught an "impersonal" humanity of Christ. Hypostasis did not mean what we call "personality." Our modern concept of personality would have to find its place, if read back into patristic anthropology, within Christ's human "nature." Cf. the further discussion of this doctrine in the third section of this chapter.

[9] The relevant texts for Leontius have been translated in The Library of Christian Classics, Vol. III, pp. 376 f. The formulation of John of Damascus is in his De orth. fide, III, ix (in MPG, 94, 1015-18).

communion of "natures" was held to be inseparable and indivisible (following the Alexandrian emphasis), and yet the two
"natures" did not lose their identity or become mixed (satisfy-
ing the Antiochene concern). The union was conceived as
neither temporary nor accidental. It was the permanent and real
result of an irreversible act of God the Word. On the other
hand, neither did the Logos cease to be God—it was not transformed and lost none of its divine glory—nor did the human
"nature" cease to be that of man or become absorbed into the
divine. This union was grounded in the one hypostasis of the
Logos. The human "nature," considered separately and therefore theoretically (apart from the fact that it was the human
"nature" of the incarnate Word), had no hypostasis of its own.
Considered concretely and actually, the humanity of Jesus had
its existence in that of the Logos.

Stated in this way, almost without interpretation, the significance of developed patristic Christology is not easy to grasp. It
has been argued that as Westerners, we tend to see these formulae of the Eastern Church as explicit and exhaustive definitions, because we use formulae in this way.[10] The Eastern mind,
we are told, has never wanted to trust in definitions. The formula is important, it is said, not as a definition, but only as an
indication of where the Fathers understood the mystery to lie,
serving also to defend the mystery against those who would
dissolve it into too-neat formulae of their own. This may be
true and it reminds us that our own way of thinking is not
universal. But the fact remains that we are Westerners, and it is
we who wish to understand what was meant by this ancient
Christology. Our difficulty in grasping the significance of these
formulae lies precisely in the fact that we are far removed from
the world of thought in which this Christology took shape.
Nevertheless, we shall try to understand it, by turning to the
interpretation of those who have sought to comprehend it

sympathetically. Criticism comes all too easily and it will find its place in due course.

Evaluations of Chalcedon

The present state of Christology is partly determined by the depreciation of patristic theology in the work of Albrecht Ritschl and his school, whose most illustrious figure was the historian Adolf von Harnack. Through these men, there has come into our time a thesis which has helped shape the contemporary problem of Christology, both for theologians and for less-sophisticated Christians. It may be summarized by saying that the original, dynamic, historical faith of the early Church, expressed in the writings of the New Testament, became "Hellenized" as the Church moved into the Hellenistic world. The Gospel, according to the Ritschlians, was transformed and deformed into a static, speculative, metaphysical theory about the person of Christ and the Godhead. The task of modern theology was to return to the dynamic, historical, Hebraic form of thought and to abandon the hopelessly metaphysical thought of the Church Fathers, who were responsible for the dogmas of Christology.

With varying emphasis, this thesis has dominated Christological discussion in our century and is still influential, not least among Christians who have never heard of Ritschl and Harnack. Its influence is evident in such common assertions as: "Hebraic thinking, which was that of Jesus and the apostles, is dynamic and historical, whereas Greek thought, such as that of the Fathers, is static and metaphysical"; "The 'Jesus of history' is one thing, the 'Christ of faith' another"; "The question of faith is not what Jesus is 'in himself,' but what he is 'for me.' " The result has been a widespread depreciation of the classical formulations of Christology.

One of the earlier writings of William Temple, later Archbishop of Canterbury, provides an example of this depreciation.

Although Temple's judgment became more conservative with time, he was clearly under the influence of the Ritschlian thesis when he wrote his article on "The Divinity of Christ," published in *Foundations* in 1912; "The formula of Chalcedon," he wrote, "is, in fact, a confession of the bankruptcy of Greek Patristic Theology. The Fathers had done the best that could be done with the intellectual apparatus at their disposal." And again, "That breakdown was inevitable, because the spiritual cannot be expressed in terms of substance at all. The whole of Greek Theology, noble as it is, suffers from a latent materialism; its doctrine of substance is in essence materialistic."[11] Greek thought is said to be fundamentally inappropriate to the problem at hand. The Fathers are credited with having done as well as they could under this handicap, but the implication is clear that we have better tools at our disposal. We would not contest the thesis that the manner of thought and the categories employed by the Fathers differed from those of the New Testament authors, and that we in the Western world do not think as the Greek Fathers thought in their time. As Temple remarked, "If a man can really believe in Human Nature existing as a separate and indivisible thing apart from all who have that nature, by all means let him use this conception to express the central fact of Christian experience."[12] Temple was obviously aware of the great distance between the fifth and the twentieth centuries. But the question remains whether the gap between the first century and today is any less wide. Temple's words seem to imply that there is some special affinity between the thought of the apostles and our own; it has been a tempting idea for theologians ever since the Renaissance.

A more positive evaluation of Chalcedon, and patristic Christology in general, has been made by Karl Barth, who represents a reaction to the Ritschlian devaluation of dogma. Barth learned from the sixteenth century Reformers to listen to the

[11] *Foundations*, B. H. Streeter, ed. (London: Macmillan, 1912), pp. 230 f.
[12] *Ibid.*, p. 233.

Fathers with care and attention. He would never place their teaching on a level with that of the New Testament, but he understands and commends the Fathers as helpful guides in the interpretation of the biblical witness.[13] Patristic Christology cannot be our own exegesis (which we must always make ourselves); it remains that of the Fathers; and yet in making his own interpretation, Barth has tried to remain faithful to Chalcedon and classical Christology. His aim has been to say in his own words just what the New Testament authors said in theirs, all the while learning something from the Fathers about how to read the New Testament, on the assumption that the Fathers were essentially trying to interpret the Bible.

It would take many pages to do more than summarize Barth's Christology, for his whole massive *Church Dogmatics* is really a Christology, and over six hundred pages in volumes I/2 and IV/2 are devoted explicitly to this doctrine. Barth's text is the New Testament rather than the patristic interpretation, but his primary text from the New Testament is the patristic favorite, John 1:14, "And the Word became flesh and dwelt among us." He admits that the Fathers tended to see Christology as an isolated problem rather than as a foundation upon which all theology might be based; John 1:14 was almost read as a text without a context. But Barth is also convinced that the very "theological hair-splitting" which has characterized the interpretation of that text is a sign of the seriousness with which the Fathers and, later, the Scholastics, both Catholic and Protestant, took the mystery of Jesus Christ to which that text and the whole New Testament bear witness. The task for theology and for faith is to stand before this mystery, to let its magnitude become evident, to learn from past orthodoxy how serious the question is, and then, in conversation with that past, to find

---

[13] For the following paragraphs, see Barth's *Kirchliche Dogmatik*, I/2, pp. 17 ff., 135 ff., 145 ff., 165 ff. (15 ff., 123 ff., 132 ff., 151 ff.) ; IV/1, pp. 205 ff., 251 ff. (188 ff., 228 ff.). On the function of dogma as a guide to exegesis, cf. H. Diem, *Dogmatik* (Munich: Chr. Kaiser Verlag, 1955), Chap. XI; trans. (Edinburgh: Oliver & Boyd, 1959).

words with which to give in our own time the answer of the apostles to the question of who is Jesus Christ.

As Bonhoeffer observed,[14] Barth is "still dominated" by a negative attitude toward nineteenth-century theology with its question of how we are to understand all this today. He has been content to expound the classical confession "true God and true man," the double confession that the man Jesus was and is the Word of God (God himself in his self-revelation), and that the Word of God is this man Jesus. Contrary to those who have accepted the Ritschlian thesis, Barth has attempted to handle patristic Christology with deep sympathy. The doctrine of the Incarnation, for Barth, is a sound exposition of the news that the Word of God, who is God himself, has participated fully in human existence. Without ceasing to be what he was, the Word became also man, a creature subject to the judgment of God. Barth rejects a reduction of the Gospel to the idea common to many religions of a god incarnate in some pure hero or saint. The Word became *flesh,* participating in sinful humanity, and it came to terms with sin precisely in our situation. Barth puts the primary stress on the divine hypostasis, as did the Fathers. The confession "true God and true man" does not posit God and man side-by-side; it was the Word which became flesh, not the reverse. The man Jesus came into existence because God the Word chose to make human history his business by invading it.[15] The Fathers tried to preserve this mystery in its richness with their doctrine of the two "natures" united in the one hypostasis. Barth insists more radically than the Fathers did, however, that the divine Word accepted all the consequences of his assumption of human "nature" and the whole burden of human sin. The glory of God the Word is just this, that he humbled himself even to death on the cross, and the perfection of

---

[14] *WE,* p. 221 (149).
[15] Barth's appreciative yet fresh handling of the doctrine of *enhypostasia* is typical of the way he interprets patristic theology. *Op. cit.,* I/2, pp. 178 ff. (163 ff.), and especially IV/2, pp. 52 f., 99 ff. (49 f., 90 ff.).

Jesus lay not in his supposed "sinproof" nature, but in his compassion for and solidarity with sinners.

This summary of Barth's Christology is sufficient to show the contrast of his approach with that of Temple in *Foundations*. Arnold Gilg also has protested, as a historian of dogma, the pervasive, uncritical acceptance of the Ritschlian thesis, arguing for an appreciation of the breadth and depth of the patristic understanding of Jesus Christ.[16] In the hands of Barth and Gilg, the Fathers are presented at their most attractive, though not without criticism, and many have learned a new appreciation of classical Christology from these men.

The Fathers developed their Christology as a message of salvation for men longing for deliverance from a world of finitude, suffering, death, and decay. If one makes allowance for the mythological world view of ancient man, which the Fathers shared with the authors of the New Testament, the work of the first four centuries of theology may be respected as a serious attempt to guard and pass on the mystery of God's entry into the world of men for their salvation. They were by no means merely trying to solve the logical problem of speaking of the union of God and man without denying either side or the unity. The union had to do with the whole cosmos, God, man, nature, and the world, and so it was to be both confessed and adored. Creation had fallen under the power of death and corruption, and now, out of his love for his creatures, God himself had entered into man's deplorable situation. His mighty Word had gone forth and brought into being one piece of a new order: a man born miraculously to be the bearer of the eternal Logos, from which all things had their being. As Athanasius put it in an analogy, it was as if a king had come to a city and had taken up residence in one of its houses. Forever after, not just that one house but the whole city could claim the honor and protection of the royal presence.[17] So God the Word had visited men in the

---

[16] Gilg, *op. cit.*
[17] *De incarn.* 9.

body of one of them and, by overcoming death and raising that one into the realm of the incorruptible, had assured the way into that realm for all the rest.

Viewed in this way, patristic Christology becomes more understandable. The Incarnation had to include a whole man, and it had to be the action of nothing less than the very Word of God, God himself. The union had to be unqualified, however distinct the "natures" were. The incorruptible God could not suffer, and yet the death on the cross had to be that death which men feared. Both "natures" had to be whole and complete, and the union had to be perfect, lest the mystery of salvation be denied.

One can go this far toward a sympathetic understanding of the thought of another age, but the fact remains that these thoughts are those of the Fathers in their own time. Their Christology was their own interpretation of the message of the New Testament. Even if it is taken at its best and with all possible sympathy, however, it is not free of problems for us, and we shall consider these problems now.

The Problem of Patristic and Biblical Categories

Considered from a modern perspective, orthodox patristic Christology did not do justice to the manhood of Jesus of Nazareth. While professing on the one hand that Jesus Christ was "very man," it defined that manhood so as to threaten the place of Jesus of Nazareth in the world of men. The problem can be seen as early as the writings of Justin Martyr, where the author insisted that Jesus was full man, with body, soul, and spirit, and yet without historical relationship to the rest of mankind, because of his miraculous birth and involvement with the Logos. He was one *like* us, but he was not one *of* us. He was a man because he had the body and soul and spirit of a man. Justin's Christ is like a specimen on the anatomist's dissecting table. It is opened to see that all the parts are there. All the parts are found, and the specimen is judged to be a fair representative of the species in question.

What is it to be a man, not to speak of "true" or perfect man? If man is to be considered on the model of a machine, or as a purely biological organism composed of certain parts, Justin's approach to the idea of perfect manhood will do. But this Christology was developed by men who professed to see in Jesus the revelation of true manhood, and the New Testament picture should have led them to see him as a man of compassion, involved in the affairs of men, characterized precisely by that which Justin did not seem to see: his relationship with other men. It is a mark of the great difference of the world of the Fathers from that of such a sympathetic modern interpreter as Barth, that what they neglected has become for him and many others the very center of a theological understanding of the manhood of Jesus of Nazareth. Certainly patristic anthropology differed from ours today, and this difference produced a different reading of the New Testament witness to Jesus of Nazareth.

In rejecting the teaching of Apollinaris, the Fathers rejected, at least by implication (and in later centuries it became explicit), all efforts to distinguish Jesus from other men on the basis of his human "nature." They maintained that he was a man like ourselves, one who could call us his brothers. Yet their formula of two "natures" united in the one hypostasis of the Logos, led to the conclusion that Jesus did not have a human hypostasis. All other men have their human "nature" and share this with Jesus Christ, but he alone had no human hypostasis. According to John of Damascus, no "nature" can be without a hypostasis, but it is not necessary that an entity have its own independent hypostasis. It may share the hypostasis of another entity, and this was the case of the humanity of the Incarnate Word. The man Jesus had his own human "nature," but his hypostasis was that of the divine Logos. The significance of this doctrine depends on how we understand the Greek term. *Hypo-*

stasis may be translated as *actuality*. Barth, following the suggestion of the Leiden Synopsis, has translated it as "existence."[18] To speak of a human hypostasis is to speak of the actual existing of a man, or, more specifically, of that which gives him his actual and independent existence. According to orthodox patristic Christology, this is what we have and which Jesus lacked, the lack being compensated by the existence of God the Word in him, which gave him his existence as a man.

Insofar as hypostasis is interpreted in this way, pointing not to some quality in Jesus but rather to the ground of his existence, insofar as this doctrine means that he was in all respects a man, differing from others solely in that his historical existence depended upon God's decision to be among men in this way, to that extent the true manhood of Jesus appears to be maintained. It is questionable whether the doctrine has really meant this, however. Christians have hesitated to say that Jesus was "only a man," even if a man whose very existence was grounded quite particularly in the existence and act of God the Word. He seems to have been considered by orthodox Christology to be qualitatively different from other men, in spite of its protestations to the contrary, so that even the most sympathetic interpretation of this doctrine does not solve the problem. Our condition as men is that of beings who have our own hypostasis, whose existence in history is, apart from what may be said by the doctrine of creation and providence, grounded in history. According to orthodox classical Christology, Jesus did not share this condition. He entered into the place where we are, but he was not grounded in this place as we are. He was a visitor, not a member of the family. In this respect, orthodox classical Christology is inadequate to meet its own goals.

The patristic conception of man was modeled on the patristic picture of the process of nature. Suffering involved change, and to change was to decay. When modern theologians define the

---

[18] Cf. note 15, *supra*.

humanity of Jesus as his being-for-others, his involvement with and compassion for his fellow men, they speak as men who are interested in history and find it a more helpful paradigm than nature for understanding man.[19] The "Jesus of history" movement of the nineteenth and early twentieth centuries was partly a result of the peculiar modern interest in history itself. From this modern perspective, we should say that the Greek Fathers tended to neglect history, as is evident in their tendency to focus, not on the incarnation as an event, but on *incarnatedness* as a condition. The debates and conclusions centered on the end terms "Word" and "flesh." The Johannine "became" was relatively untouched. In this connection, the Ritschlian thesis points to one truth: patristic thought tended to be static.

The rejection of the proposal of Paul of Samosata to consider the christological problem in terms other than those of the Word incarnate in flesh, illustrates this static tendency. What Paul actually proposed was admittedly inadequate. A picture of Jesus slowly becoming ever more closely united to God through obedience until finally rewarded with adoption, is not only without historical foundations or textual support; it also represents a naïve conception of the interrelationship of freedom and destiny in human life, to use Paul Tillich's terms.[20] It is conducive to a moralistic interpretation of Jesus. Yet the door need not have been closed on the alternative suggested by Paul without exploring its promise and possibilities. The promise lay in its suggestion of a more historical conception of Jesus and of the whole relationship of God and man in Jesus' history. In stressing the obedience of Jesus, Paul was not only on good exegetical ground, but he was affirming a perspective which, by taking one piece of history seriously, might have led to taking all history seriously. Moreover, in basing the union between

---

[19] On the distinction between nature and history, cf. R. G. Collingwood, *The Idea of History* (New York: Oxford University Press, 1956); and R. R. Niebuhr, *Resurrection and Historical Reason* (New York: Scribner, 1957).

[20] *Systematic Theology*, Vol. II (Chicago: University of Chicago Press, 1957), pp. 62 ff., 149.

Jesus and the one he called Father on his obedience, he was interpreting the involvement of God in history in personal and dynamic terms, an interpretation which has found many sympathizers in modern times.[21]

The patristic idea of God colored the whole development of classical Christology and has posed a problem for theology ever since. The Fathers insisted at all costs on the impassibility of God and his Word, for change was the mark of the imperfect, the sign of corruption and decay. This is a difficult presupposition with which to expound the biblical writings, however. On the one hand, the Fathers said that God was in Christ in an indissoluble union with Christ's human "nature." On the other hand, they said that Jesus Christ had actually suffered and died on the cross. If they had been more consistent in saying that God is unknown apart from his self-revelation and that we must begin with Jesus Christ in order to know anything about God at all, they might have been able to begin with the cross as the event of self-revelation of a God who is quite able to take suffering to himself and whose glory is so great that he can also humble himself. Had this been done, the course of the development of classical Christology would have been quite different.[22] But except for one passage in the writings of Gregory of Nyssa,[23] there is no sign that any of the Greek Fathers saw even the possibility of opening up the christological problem in this way, and the whole history of orthodox theology, Protestant as well as Catholic, has continued in their line.

The Fathers intended, nevertheless, to be true to the Bible, for it was their canon, their norm. Their Christologies, the one finally formulated at Chalcedon and also the rejected alternatives, were meant to be faithful to the New Testament witness. Of course, they made their own interpretation, which was

[21] Cf. Temple, *op. cit.*, pp. 226 f., typical of the widespread Ritschlian interest in Paul of Samosata's proposal.

[22] Cf. van Buren, *Christ in Our Place* (Edinburgh: Oliver & Boyd, 1957), pp. 12 f., 22 f., 141.

[23] *Logos kat.* 24. Trans. in *Library of Christian Classics*, Vol. III, pp. 300 f.

neither that of the apostles nor one which we can simply adopt today. They made the Gospel their own, because they were convinced that it was for the Greeks as well as for the Jews, for the fifth century as well as for the first. For this they are to be commended rather than criticized, even if their formulations cannot be ours, and for a similar reason: the twentieth century is not the fifth. If the Gospel is also for empirical, industrial, Western man in our time, then it is not a lack of loyalty to the Fathers which leads contemporary theologians to make their own interpretation of Christ, rather than simply repeating the words of the Fathers. Before we come to a contemporary interpretation of Christology, however, we shall do well to identify the major themes of the Gospel which the Fathers intended to express with their Christology. In speaking of the Fathers here we refer not only to those theologians who came after and defended Athanasius, but also to all those who later appealed to Athanasius and his followers as the norm of orthodoxy and who supported the "orthodox" notion that the Fathers had a single christological mind.

First of all, the Fathers believed there was one God and one history of revelation, and their Christology expressed this conviction. This one God was known through his self-revelation, in the Law and the Prophets, and then finally and fully in Jesus Christ. The Johannine assertion (John 14:9), that he who had seen Jesus had seen the Father, formulates a major New Testament theme which was also crucial for the Fathers: Jesus as the full and adequate revelation of God. He who saw and heard Jesus, saw and heard God. Jesus was the very Word of God himself, spoken into the midst of this world. Although the Fathers missed something of the dynamic, historical note of this theme and worked with categories which seem too static or metaphysical, they took seriously this central affirmation of the New Testament.

Patristic Christology, however, emphasized that in Jesus Christ there was not only divine revelation, but also a divine action. The Fathers also affirmed this related theme of the kerygma: "in Christ God was reconciling the world to himself" (II Cor. 5:19). They insisted that that which had taken place in the life, death, and resurrection of Jesus was an act of God himself.

In order to make these assertions unequivocally clear, the Fathers finally rejected all attempts to qualify them. They insisted on the one hand that the Son, or Word of God, was consubstantial with the Father, lest it be suggested that in seeing him, we see anything less than the Father, the very heart of God. Everything which was to be ascribed to the Father, other than his peculiar relationship to the Son, was also to be ascribed to that Son, himself eternal, pre-existent, very God of very God. On the other hand, they asserted the incarnation of this Son in a full and complete man, lest it be thought that God's work with respect to this one man might not be effective for all other men. Certain problems in this part of their teaching have already been pointed out, but given the terms in which they thought, their solution was perhaps the best that could be found. Finally, they insisted on a full and perfect unity of the divine and human "natures," lest this act of God's be thought to be temporary or partial. The unity, they maintained, was in the hypostasis of the Logos, lest it be suggested that there was anything accidental or contingent about that saving event. It was the act of God himself, they insisted, which excluded any understanding of the saving event as a co-operative undertaking by God and man. It was an act of grace, not dependent upon man. The "natures" were united inseparably and indivisibly, they maintained, for this act was final and eternal, but they insisted also that the two "natures" remained unchanged and unmixed, lest the obedience of Jesus and the involvement of man and God in this event seem to be artificial. Each aspect of classical Christology expresses the patristic concern to interpret and preserve the apostolic witness without dilution.

There can be little doubt that the thought and categories of the Fathers are quite different from ours. The Ritschlian thesis, however, asserts that the thought world of the Fathers is also far from that of the New Testament. The wide acceptance of this judgment, and of the assumption that we can more easily understand the thought of the biblical writers than that of the Fathers, has contributed to the rise of modern "biblical theology." Whether biblical theology does in fact understand the thought world of the Bible better than did the Fathers is perhaps a judgment best left to history. In any case, biblical theology has given modern theology a fresh appreciation of the distinctive thought world of the Bible and of the categories which were central for the biblical authors.[24] The centrality of the Covenant, the highly dynamic, historical character of the event of God's self-revelation, the importance of obedience as the proper response of man in God's Covenant, are biblical categories which played only a minor part in the development of patristic Christology. By using these categories, contemporary theology has developed another Christology, which shares, nevertheless, the concerns and intentions of the Fathers.

The central theme of the whole biblical witness is the Covenant of God with Israel. We have learned today how this one theme controlled the way in which Israel took over and refashioned such ancient myths as those of creation and the fall of man.[25] It was the basis of the whole tradition of revealed law, and it was the hinge on which the prophetic message turned. It was the central motif in Israel's worship as reflected in the Psalms, and its fulfillment was the hope of her apocalytic writers. The New Testament has presented the message and mission of Jesus as the fulfillment and renewal of the Covenant, and the

[24] But for a critique of the linguistic assumption of such monuments of biblical theology as the *Theologisches Wörterbuch zum Neuen Testament* and of the current fashion of drawing a sharp line between Greek and Hebrew thought on linguistic grounds, see J. Barr, *The Semantics of Biblical Language* (London: Oxford University Press, 1961).

[25] Cf. G. von Rad, *ATD, Das erste Buch Mose* (Göttingen: Vandenhoeck & Ruprecht, 1953), pp. 7-13, 15 f. Translated by John H. Marks, *Genesis: a commentary* (London: SCM Press, 1961).

traditional titles of the two parts of the Bible are appropriately "The Old Covenant" and "The New Covenant."[26] If we are concerned with the question of God and man, their separation and reconciliation, and if we are content to understand these in the terms of biblical thought (however foreign this may be for us today and however approximate a contemporary grasp of the thought of such a distant era must be), the idea of the Covenant seems to offer a promising framework within which to work.

The Covenant was made between two parties, and these parties are always presented in the biblical documents as they were involved in this relationship. God was not simply God; he was the God who made his Covenant with Israel. He was the God who had chosen this people, the electing God, and not their possession (though Israel often acted as if he were). And Israel was not simply Israel, but always the people on whom God had set his love, not for their own sake simply (though Israel often acted as if this too were the case), but for the sake of the world. Israel was brought into historical existence by the Covenant which God had made with them. The first question for Israel was therefore always the question of faithfulness to the God of the Covenant. Finally, the goal of this Covenant was God's gracious plan for the whole world. If obedience meant being free for God, it meant also being free for the world, free to serve it, to bear witness to it, and to be "a light to the nations" (Isa. 49:6).

The contention of the theological "right" that patristic Christology is an interpretation of the New Testament, though not the only possible one, may be illuminated by comparing this Christology with a modern interpretation developed on the paradigm of the Covenant.[27] An interpretation so developed

----

[26] The Covenant has been used before as a key concept for theology, in the federal theology, so-called, usually associated with J. Cocceius, one of its chief proponents, which was influential in the Reformed theology of the seventeenth century. What we are developing here is quite different. For a critical note on federal theology, see P. Miller, *The New England Mind, The Seventeenth Century* (Cambridge, Mass.: Harvard University Press, 1954), pp. 365 ff., 502 ff.

[27] Cf. note 25, p. 18, *supra.*

will involve reading passages such as John 1:14 against their background in the Old Testament, rather than through the eyes, and with the categories, of the Fathers. Nevertheless, such a Christology can be faithful to the intentions of the Fathers and also represent the thinking of theologians of the "right" who have been influenced by the insights of biblical theology.

A Christology of "Call" and "Response"

Theological tradition has such a hold on Christians that they are inclined to read the words of the New Testament in the light of their later theological use. This is especially true of such words as "God," "Son of God," and "Christ," and we must specify how these words will be used in the following interpretation of the New Testament witness to Jesus. When the Old Testament authors spoke of God, they meant Yahweh, the God of Sinai, the God of the Covenant, the God of Abraham, Isaac, and Jacob. Whatever variation there may have been originally in these various designations, clarity may be obtained by using the name "Yahweh" instead of speaking of "God," for the New Testament authors never had any other God in mind than the God of the Old Testament. Confusion has also centered on the word "Christ," which was first a title and then became used as part of a proper name, perhaps even before the end of the New Testament period. Since it was originally a title of office, it implies something more than a different form of the name "Jesus." The ambiguous word "Christ" may be avoided by referring to the central figure of the Gospels as "Jesus" or "Jesus of Nazareth." The office or title "Christ" may be indicated by the Hebrew word "Messiah."

Finally, the title "Son" or "Son of God" needs clarification because of the role it played in the development of classical Christology. The title "Son," or more fully "Son of God," is applied frequently to Jesus in the New Testament, but the term is one with a long history hardly compatible with the way in which it was used by the Fathers. The title "Son," according to biblical scholars, was used in the Old Testament first as a designation for Israel and then as a designation for those who specially represented the people of the Covenant, such as the king or the high priest. The title implied serving obedience. Oscar Cullmann has written that this term was used in the Old Testament and in Judaism in a way "essentially characterized, not by the gift of a particular power, nor by a substantial relationship with God by virtue of divine conception, but by the idea of election to participation in divine work through the execution of a particular commission and by the idea of strict obedience to the God who elects."[28] The context of this thought is the fact that the primitive Christian community "as a matter of course applied to Jesus passages from the Old Testament which referred to Israel."[29] In calling him the Son of God, the apostolic community was saying that the true and faithful Israel had come. God had chosen him as his *servant*[30] to participate in his plan for the world, to be (as the old Israel had not been willing to be) "a light to lighten the Gentiles." Jesus as "Son of God" meant Jesus as the obedient bearer of a specific election or commission. This title, interpreted by its use in the Old Testament, provides a basis from which to develop a Christology of "call" and "response."

A beginning may be made by looking at two passages in the Gospel of John which appear to support patristic Christology, because they have been read for so long through the eyes of the Fathers and in the light of their Logos interpretation. If these passages are examined with the paradigm of the Covenant in mind, however, it becomes evident that there is more than one way of reading them. The first of these passages is John 9:29-33,

[28] Oscar Cullmann, *The Christology of the New Testament* (London: SCM Press Ltd., 1959), p. 275.

[29] E. Schweizer, *Lordship and Discipleship* (Naperville, Ill.: Allenson's, 1960), p. 43.

[30] Attention is called to this early designation of Jesus in the sermon and prayers in Acts 3:13, 26; 4:25, 27, 30.

which reports a dispute between some Pharisees and a man
born blind whom Jesus had healed. The passage opens with the
Pharisees speaking:

> 'We know that God has spoken to Moses, but as for this
> man [Jesus] we do not know where he comes from.' The man
> answered, 'Why this is a marvel! You do not know where he
> comes from, and yet he opened my eyes. We know that God
> does not listen to sinners, but if anyone is a worshipper of
> God and does his will, God listens to him. Never since the
> world began has it been heard that any one opened the eyes
> of a man born blind. If this man were not from God, he
> could do nothing.'

In this comparison of Jesus with Moses, some interesting expressions are used. Moses is characterized as a man to whom God
"has spoken." It is also said that God listens to "any one who is
a worshipper of God and does his will." Finally, it is asserted that
Jesus could do nothing if he were not "from God." This last
expression is particularly interesting, for we tend, following
patristic Christology, to assume that such expressions as "from
God" and "sent by God" refer to the coming of the Logos from
the bosom of Yahweh "down" into this world. But although the
expression "from God" refers explicitly to Jesus, it is implicitly
applicable to Moses. To be "from God" is to be a man to whom
God has spoken and who is obedient to Yahweh's will.

This interpretation is supported by a passage in the next
chapter, reporting the final dispute between Jesus and his enemies, which arose from Jesus' claim to be one with the Father
(John 10:30-38):

> 'I and the Father are one.' The Jews took up stones
> again to stone him. Jesus answered them, 'I have shown you
> many good works from the Father; for which of these do you
> stone me?' The Jews answered him, 'We stone you for no
> good work but for blasphemy; because you, being a man,
> make yourself God.' Jesus answered them, 'Is it not written

in your law, "I said, you are gods"? If he called them gods
to whom the word of God came (and scripture cannot be
broken), do you say of him whom the Father consecrated
and sent into the world, "You are blaspheming," because I
said, "I am the Son of God"? If I am not doing the works of
my Father, then do not believe me; but if I do them, even
though you do not believe me, believe the works, that you
may know and understand that the Father is in me and I am
in the Father.'

In the answer to the charge of "the Jews," another series of
interesting expressions is used. Jesus says that to be one with the
Father, or to be "in the Father" and to have the Father "in"
him, is the same as to be the "Son of God." But to be the "Son
of God" is to do "the works of my Father" and to be one to
whom the "word of God" has come, referring to Ps. 82:6. It
means being commissioned by God and being obedient to that
commission or consecration. The phrase "consecrated and sent
into the world" seems to be a clear support for a Christology of
incarnation of the divine Logos, but when it is read in the light
of the concept of the Covenant, with Jesus in the role of Israel,
another interpretation is possible. "Consecrated and sent into
the world" can refer as clearly to the earthly calling and mission
of Jesus as it can to a heavenly consecration and an incarnation.
If it is taken in this way, however, the weaknesses of the "adoption" Christology and how they are to be met will have to be
considered with care, but those weaknesses need not disqualify
this alternative to the incarnational Christology of the Fathers.

This second passage poses a problem for the Logos Christology of the Fathers. Who is speaking here? If it is Jesus, as the
evangelist asserts, then this passage says that it is the Father who
is "in" Jesus, not the Logos. If it is the divine Logos speaking,
then the figure of Jesus of Nazareth is reduced to a puppet.
Whichever way one takes it, the passage begs for some other
interpretation.

By using the paradigm of the Covenant, Jesus of Nazareth

is seen here as a man called to a particular role in history by Yahweh for the sake of the world. If we begin with this election, we may do justice to what Tillich has called the element of destiny, which is always in polarity with freedom. We may also avoid the difficulty of Paul of Samosata, who seems to have begun with the man Jesus and then tried to understand a relationship between this man and Yahweh. Yahweh's election of Jesus as the expression of his will and purpose is the starting point for a better interpretation. In the New Testament, this election is called "eternal," which means that Yahweh's whole plan and purpose was involved in this choice. Since the calling of Jesus to be Yahweh's Israel for the world has led to the fulfillment of the Covenant, it is regarded by New Testament authors as prior to the call of old Israel, prior in order, evidently, since it is obviously not prior in time:

> "Blessed be the God and Father of our Lord Jesus Christ, who . . . chose us in him before the foundation of the world. . . . He has made known to us in all wisdom and insight the mystery of his will, according to his purpose which he set forth in Christ as a plan for the fullness of time, to unite all things in him, things in heaven and things on earth" (Ephesians 1:3, 4, 9, 10).

This passage leads us to say that the election of Jesus of Nazareth to be supremely the man who lived for the sake of other men was Yahweh's primary decision, which began to be realized in the creation of the world and then in the calling of Israel. It was finally enacted in Jesus, and its consummation is the Christian hope. The apostolic witness will not allow us to say of this decision that "there was a time when it was not." It is an abstraction to conceive of Yahweh in any other way than as the one who has made himself known through his covenant with Jesus for the sake of the world. As the Old Testament community looked back and retold popular myths of creation in the light of Sinai and the Red Sea deliverance, so the New Testament community looked back not only to creation but to the whole history of the Covenant and retold it all in the light of Jesus of Nazareth, Yahweh's faithful new Israel, the Son of God.

Yahweh's decision expresses his very heart. The prologue of the Gospel of John summarizes this idea by saying that God's word is God himself, from the "beginning." It was possible to identify Yahweh with his decision because the New Testament authors conceived of God always in relation to the decision enacted in Jesus of Nazareth. In the beginning there was the decision that there should be one for the many, and that the many should come to know themselves to be involved with the one. And "in the fullness of time," this purpose was enacted concretely in the history of Jesus of Nazareth. It became flesh, a plan enacted, and Yahweh's purpose dwelt among us in that Jesus dwelt among men. What Yahweh had to say to man, what he had in mind for men, was to be heard and seen in the form of this man, who was, therefore, the very word of Yahweh.

So long as a word is not thought of as an ideal entity, but as an action leading to a relationship, the assertion that the Word actually became Jesus does not involve us in the pagan idea of a transmutation of the divine into the physical.[31] An intention became an action; a plan was enacted. To ask whether the plan exists apart from its enactment, or whether it has been transformed into its enactment, indicates that one is thinking of a plan or a word as a quasi-physical substance. It is simply a plan, and its enactment is simply what results when the plan is realized. To summarize this idea in naïve terms, Yahweh determined in his heart of hearts upon having his faithful son, Jesus, and through him a faithful creation. He created this world and called his people Israel for this purpose. He realized this purpose concretely in history when he called this man into

[31] In order to avoid the idea of transmutation, Tillich proposes the alternate course of not stressing the verb in the Johannine, "the Word became flesh." *Systematic Theology*, Vol. II, p. 149.

a role in history upon which he had decided "before the foundation of the world." This leads to the other side of Christology, which the later Fathers designated with the term "human nature," and which, as we have noted, was always a weak point in their doctrine. We said that Jesus was called to a particular role in history as the concrete realization of Yahweh's purpose for man, but this does not mean that he was in any way other-than-human. However "conceived by the Holy Spirit, born of the virgin Mary" is to be understood, it ought not to threaten the idea that Jesus was a human being like ourselves. The nativity stories express wonder at the appearance in history of the man of Yahweh's good pleasure, whose very advent was, poetically speaking, cause for celestial signs and angelic hymns. Indeed, his birth *was* unique, for it was the birth of the man who fulfilled Israel's role. His uniqueness, however, did not make him "more than a man," whatever that would be; the uniqueness of Jesus of Nazareth, according to the witness of the New Testament, consisted in his being the man who bore a particular calling from Yahweh, to which he responded in his own particular history. According to the New Testament witness, Jesus' history was that of perfect obedience to his calling, even to the point of his death on a cross.

The apostolic witnesses made no attempt to account for Jesus' obedience. Rather, they stood in awe before this obedience, which was authenticated for them by the Easter event. There is no external criterion by which we might see whether Jesus was in fact obedient. Easter was taken to be Yahweh's proclamation of this obedience (Rom. 1:4), and the Easter Gospel of the disciples was the expression of their conviction that Jesus of Nazareth was Yahweh's Israel by calling and by his faithful obedience.

When we compare this interpretation with that of the Fathers, we find that it meets the problems which led the Fathers to their conclusions. The patristic Logos or Eternal Son has been interpreted as Yahweh's purpose, the expression of his very self, and as such it meets the problem posed by Arianism. The Fathers wanted to say "God of God," and in our own way we have said the same. They said that Jesus Christ was "very man," and we have secured this side of the matter in another way: we have conceived of the fullness or perfection of man as residing not in the fact that all of his "parts" are there, but in his historical existence and social relationships. We may say that Jesus was thoroughly and willingly involved in history and in relationships with others, with friends and enemies, socially and politically. He was truly man in that he was as involved in life, as mixed up in politics, as much in the middle of human hate and love, friendship and enmity, as it is possible for man to be, and he was like this in fulfilling his calling to be present for others.

A response must follow and depend upon a call. This logic underlies our interpretation of the doctrine of the enhypostatic character of the man Jesus. So entirely is he to be understood from the perspective of Easter, so fully is his life to be seen as a life of obedience to a divine election, that, like the New Testament, the believer cannot speak of a Jesus of Nazareth who might have existed independently of Yahweh's purpose. This man, moreover, though fully man and in no sense "more than a man," is not to be confused with other men. He stood apart from them for the very reason of his solidarity with them: he was the one man who truly existed for others. His calling was to be the one for the many, whereas the calling of all other men is to let him be that for them: the way, the truth, and the life. He stands apart from all the others also in that he was obedient to his calling, whereas they are not obedient to theirs, or they only learn obedience by relying solely on the obedience of him whom they know and confess as Lord and Saviour.

This interpretation of Jesus and the Gospel is an example of the kind of Christology which is being developed in many quarters by men influenced by biblical theology, and it is intended to be faithful to the concerns evident in the Christology of the Fathers. We have presented that tradition and suggested this contemporary interpretation of it in order to make clear what conservative theology has held to be the constituent elements of the Gospel. At the center stands the person of Jesus of Nazareth. But although such an interpretation may be called "orthodox," it is still, from the point of view of the theological "left," sadly mythological in form, if not in content.

III

THE CONCERN

FOR UNDERSTANDING

Existentialist Interpretations of a
Gospel without Myth

A contemporary understanding of the Gospel has been the particular concern of the theological "left." Having considered the christological concern of conservative theologians in the last chapter, we turn now to the desire of liberal theologians to find a more understandable expression of the Gospel. Rudolf Bultmann epitomizes this concern, but Schubert Ogden is a more useful example, because he represents the position which arises from the fear that even Bultmann has not gone far enough in making the Gospel available to contemporary man. By analyzing his argument with Bultmann and his own alternative, we shall see the merits of the position of the "left," and discover how adequate it is to the task of interpreting the Gospel in a secular age: whether it does justice to the Gospel, on the one hand, or to the way in which we think today, on the other.

We shall begin with Ogden's analysis of Bultmann's proposal. According to both men, the basic problem for modern man in understanding the New Testament is that he can no longer accept the mythological world-picture in which the New Testament message is clothed. " 'A mythological world-picture' is one in which (1) the nonobjective reality that man experiences as the ground and limit of himself and his world is 'objectified' and thus presented as but another part of the objective world; (2) the origin and goal of the world as a whole, as well as certain happenings within it, are referred to nonnatural, yet 'objective' causes; (3) the resulting complex of ideas comprising the picture takes the form of a double history."[1] The New Testament pictures the world as having three stories. Heaven, which signifies the transcendent, is conceived spatially as being "above" the earth. The New Testament "objectifies" heaven by representing it as a sphere "within the inclusive world of objective reality."[2] The world is thought to have originated in a supernatural act, and supposed interventions of the divine in this world are almost commonplace in the biblical documents. Finally, a superhuman, divine history runs parallel to human history. Ogden points out that Bultmann has defined myth carefully. A concept of a three-storied universe is only a bit of primitive science. What makes this primitive science mythological in the New Testament is the belief that the upper and lower realms are transcendent. The heart of Bultmann's definition lies in the idea of *objectification* of "the nonobjective reality that man experiences as the ground and limit of himself and his world."

Bultmann admits that superstition and remnants of prescientific thinking (such as belief in miracles of healing) may still be found today, but he says they are exceptions to the clear trend of twentieth-century thought. Modern man cannot recon-

[1] Ogden, *op. cit.*, p. 27. Ogden gives detailed references in his study to Bultmann's writings. Citations from Bultmann will be given only when I wish to refer to some point not clear from the references in Ogden's book, or when I prefer to make my own translation. Otherwise, I will simply refer to Ogden, since his interpretation of Bultmann is acceptable for our purposes.
[2] *Ibid.*

cile the New Testament picture of man in the control of demons or spirits with his understanding of himself as a free, responsible being, nor can he understand how the death and supposed resurrection long ago of a divine figure can have any effect upon him and his destiny. "The only divine speaking and acting [modern man] can understand as important and of concern to him are such as encounter him in his personal existence."[3]

One motive for Bultmann's program, then, is the desire to make the Gospel understandable to, and thus unavoidable for, modern man. Another motive is Bultmann's belief that the biblical myths did not arise in order to paint a certain picture of the world, but to express "how man understands himself in his world."[4] Behind the mythology lay an understanding of man. New Testament mythology expresses the believer's understanding that he is not lord over himself, and that his freedom from such forces as selfishness and despair lies in his dependence on transcendent powers, which exist beyond the known world and constitute its ground and limit.[5] Myth is therefore not simply to be eliminated; it must be interpreted as an expression of man's existential self-understanding.

Bultmann is convinced that the New Testament not only allows but demands this interpretation. There are basically only two kinds of statements, he believes: those which give information, and those which demand a decision of the listener or reader;[6] those of the kerygma are of the second type. They demand that the reader decide how he shall understand himself. According to Ogden, "Bultmann reduced the entire contents of the traditional Christian confession to one fundamental assertion: *I henceforth understand myself no longer in terms of my past, but solely in terms of the future that is here and now disclosed to me as grace in my encounter with the church's*

3 *Ibid.*, p. 171.
4 *Ibid.*, p. 39.
5 *Ibid.*, pp. 39 f.
6 *Ibid.*, p. 50. Ogden argues that this is assumed in all of Bultmann's writings.

proclamation."[7] The kerygma tells man that he may understand himself in this way, and the response of faith is the affirmation of this self-understanding. The very nature of the New Testament witness and of faith, therefore, demands an existentialist interpretation. To treat the New Testament as a source of information, and faith as assent to what is said, is to misunderstand the character of the document.

Bultmann's depends heavily on Martin Heidegger's philosophy of existence. Man is not only a being who exists, but one who knows that he exists and who can analyze the meaning of existence. Human existence is in fact characterized by a never-ending questioning by man about who he is, for man is not only related to himself; he is responsible for himself; he must make his own decision about who he is. Finally, his decision is always made in relation to his situation, so that to exist means not only to decide who he is and will be personally, but also to understand himself in relation to others and the world about him. As Ogden summarizes it, "the answer to the *existentiell* question of who one is to be always takes the form of just such a self-understanding."[8] Or again, "For man to 'exist' in the technical sense that Bultmann presupposes, means he is a being who must continually face and answer the question of what it is to be a man. It means, in a word, that he is *a moral or religious being*, one who always has to deal with the problem of what he *ought* to be."[9]

Bultmann recognizes that he may be asked: If faith is a new self-understanding in which man's original possibility of authentic existence is realized, is the historical occurrence of Jesus of Nazareth really necessary for faith? Is it not sufficient that the proclamation of the Gospel confront a man, whatever be the origin of this proclamation in a past age? An analysis of human existence can not only discover the same things that the New

---

[7] *Ibid.*, p. 114.
[8] *Ibid.*, p. 47.
[9] *Ibid.*, p. 48.

Testament says about man and his situation; it can even say what existence means.[10] Bultmann's answer is that the realization of authentic existence depends on the occurrence of Jesus. "According to the New Testament, man has lost this factual possibility [of authentic existence]; even his knowledge of his authenticity is perverted, so that he thinks it is his to command."[11] Man cannot free himself; he must be set free, and this can happen only because God has already given himself for us in Jesus Christ. This saving act of God, however, is not in the distant past, for the liberating event takes place when a man responds to the word of the cross by deciding to understand himself as crucified and dead to his own past and open solely to the future offered to him in that word. The issue of this self-understanding was posed for the disciples by their confrontation with Jesus and his message, and again by the crucifixion. The "objective fact" connected with Easter was their response of faith to God's gracious offer of this new possibility of authentic existence.[12] In other words, God's saving act really consists in having instituted the ministry of reconciliation. The Gospel itself is "the power of God for salvation to every one who has faith" (Rom. 1:16);[13] nevertheless, this Gospel arose out of the response of the first disciples to the cross and the person and words of Jesus of Nazareth. Bultmann insists upon this historical grounding of the kerygma, even though, as the *saving* event, "the cross of Christ" is the word which is proclaimed and grasped in faith here and now.

Critics to the right and left of Bultmann have seen that he tries to maintain two incompatible theses. After careful analysis of the writings of Bultmann and his critics, Ogden states Bultmann's theses as follows: " (1) Christian faith is to be interpreted exhaustively and without remainder as man's original possibility

---

[10] *Ibid.*, pp. 69 ff.
[11] Bultmann, *Kerygma und Mythos*, Vol. I, p. 39 (29).
[12] Ogden, *op. cit.*, p. 87.
[13] *Ibid.*, p. 89.

of authentic historical (*geschichtlich*) existence as this is more or less adequately clarified and conceptualized by an appropriate philosophical analysis. (2) Christian faith is actually realizable, or is a 'possibility in fact,' only because of the particular historical (*historisch*) event of Jesus of Nazareth, which is the originative event of the church and its distinctive word and sacraments."[14]

The incompatibility is evident in the double use of the word "possibility." Either faith has always been possible in fact, regardless of the appearance of Jesus of Nazareth, and every man is responsible for believing in God, or faith is not an unconditional possibility for man, and he may not be held responsible for not believing in God or charged with being without excuse (Rom. 2:1). The critics to the right and to the left disagree as to how to settle this dilemma, of course: those to the right hold for the second thesis and deny the first; those to the left make the opposite choice. Both sides agree that Bultmann's position will not do as it stands because of this inconsistency.

Ogden's first principle for a solution to this problem from the point of view of the left is that *"the demand for demythologization that arises with necessity from the situation of modern man must be accepted without condition."*[15] This normative "situation of modern man" includes contemporary man's conviction that he is responsible for himself. Since man is also addressed in the New Testament as a responsible being, he must have the possibility of authentic existence apart from the event of Jesus Christ, simply because man stands everywhere and at all times before the God of love and self-giving. Whenever he has not accepted God, he has been "without excuse." Ogden's alternative to Bultmann's first thesis, then, is: *"Christian faith is to be interpreted exhaustively and without remainder as man's original possibility of authentic existence as this is clarified*

---

14 *Ibid.*, p. 112.
15 *Ibid.*, p. 127.

and conceptualized by an appropriate philosophical analysis."[16] The omission of the words "historical" and "to be more or less" underscore Ogden's conviction that Christian faith is simply the real possibility for every man of authentic existence, which has been adequately defined by Heidegger.

This variation on Bultmann's first thesis leads Ogden to change the second thesis more radically. His alternative is: *"Christian faith is always a 'possibility in fact' because of the unconditioned gift and demand of God's love, which is the ever-present ground and end of all created things; the decisive manifestation of this divine love, however, is the event of Jesus of Nazareth, which fulfills and corrects all other manifestations and is the originative event of the church and its distinctive word and sacraments."*[17] The basic difference lies in changing "only" to "always." The particular, historical prerequisite for faith, which is the event of Jesus of Nazareth, has been replaced by a universal and omnipresent prerequisite or cause. The historical event is qualified as being "decisive" for, and "fulfilling and correcting" all other manifestations of, the universal cause. In presenting "Christ without myth," Ogden has also made room for faith without Christ, or at least without a "Christ" bound up with the historical man Jesus of Nazareth—an interesting, but not original, conclusion.

Problems of "God," Language, and History

At the beginning of his book, Ogden says that the significance of any theological statement may be tested by asking whether "the solution it actually develops is adequate, in the sense of comprehending the major dimensions that any such solution should comprehend and of being internally self-consistent."[18]

[16] *Ibid.*, p. 146.
[17] *Ibid.*, p. 153.
[18] *Ibid.*, pp. 17 f.

We take this to mean that a theological reconstruction should be not only logically consistent, but that it should also do justice to both the thinking of contemporary man and the major elements of the Gospel. According to his own criterion, Ogden's restatement seems to us to be inadequate: it does not do justice to the thinking of modern man when it speaks of "experienced nonobjective reality"; it does not see that modern man cannot even speak analogically about "God"; and it ignores the empirical aspect of statements in the kerygma. It fails also to do justice to the Gospel by neglecting the role of Jesus of Nazareth in the kerygma and the significance of Easter in the relationship between faith and Jesus. These shortcomings in the position represented by Ogden, partly inherited from Bultmann, will have to be overcome in our own and in any other alternative to Bultmann's proposal.

1. The expression "experienced nonobjective reality," as it is used by Ogden, is meaningless. If it means simply other human beings, as Ogden implies at one point, the expression is only misleading. According to Bultmann, "experienced nonobjective reality" is that which is objectified in mythological thinking. To objectify something seems to mean, at least for Ogden, speaking or conceiving of what is personal as if it were a thing, for he insists that Bultmann distinguishes the realm of the "objective" from "the realm of human existence or man's distinctively personal life."[19] If this were what Bultmann meant, then, "experienced nonobjective reality" would refer to other human beings. Certainly we experience other people, and if we wish to forget that people may also be described biologically, chemically, psychologically, and sociologically, we might, by Ogden's odd use of words, call our neighbor a "nonobjective reality." We doubt very much, however, that "modern man" would know what we were talking about if we spoke in this way, for men today do not forget that man may also be described by the natural and social sciences.

[19] *Ibid.*, p. 168.

It seems, however, that neither Ogden nor Bultmann has other human beings in mind when they speak of "experienced nonobjective reality." They seem to mean "God," or the "Transcendent," or (to use Ogden's phrase) "the unconditioned gift and demand of God's love, which is the ever-present ground and end of all created things." This is no less puzzling. This "ground and end of all created things" is said to be experienced, yet it is also called "nonobjective." This extremely odd use of the word "experience," which is ordinarily used of that which can be sensed in some way, suggests a confusion of categories, a mixing of language-games. Let us apply the verification principle to the expression: What would count for an experience being an experience of "the ground and end of all things"? In order to answer, we should first have to know what would count for something being "the ground and end of all things," or what would count against it, but there is no answer to this question. We might have an *idea* of a "ground and end of all things," and we might then have some experience which we should claim to be an experience of that of which we had an idea, but our assertions about this "ground and end" would only function by referring to how we felt about "all things." If "modern man" could make any sense of Ogden's phrase, he would have to take it as a strange way of speaking of an attitude on the part of Ogden and Bultmann. That allows the words a certain meaning, but Ogden writes as if he had something else in mind. This brings us to our second objection, which is only a more radical form of the first.

2. It is meaningless to speak analogically about God. Bultmann asserts that we may speak of "God's act" if we do so analogically, on the model of human action and encounter, although actually "an act of God is not visible to the objectifying eye and cannot be established as can worldly events."[20] He rejects a manner of speaking in which the symbol "God" refers to our own subjective experiences, but he allows that modern man could

[20] Bultmann, *Kerygma und Mythos*, Vol. II, p. 196. Cf. Ogden, *op. cit.*, p. 91.

see God's act "in an occurrence that grasped him in the reality of his own true life and transformed his own self."[21] More sharply: "Man can very well know who God is in the question concerning himself."[22] In short, Bultmann thinks that "modern man" can still do something with the word "God," that there is a way to speak of God both analogically and existentially which man today can understand. Ogden agrees with this.[23] Relying heavily on Bultmann's distinction between myth and analogy, he too believes that man today can understand himself in relationship to God, namely as a person addressed by God.

Ogden says, however, that "statements about God and his activities *are* 'statements about human existence,' and *vice versa.*"[24] Does he mean that God-statements are actually statements about man, so that when we talk about God as creator, for example, we are not really talking about any "thing," "person," or "reality" at all? Is it really only an exceedingly misleading way of saying that we have a feeling of dependence, or that we think that this world is not self-explanatory? If so, why does he add, "and *vice versa*"? When we say that we are afraid of dying, for example, by what stretch of the English language are we talking about more than our attitude? How could we be taken to be talking about "God and his activities"? Is modern man really as religiously inclined as that?

As a matter of fact, Ogden has made this assertion about theology, not about the language of modern man. At another point, however, he applies the same assertion to the language of faith generally, basing his case on the argument that "God and man are of such a nature and are so related that to speak adequately of either is in fact to speak of both."[25] Even in this limited sphere, however, can one say that one *is* the other and vice versa without hopelessly confusing the empirically-minded

21 Bultmann, *Kerygma und Mythos*, Vol. I, p. 21.
22 Bultmann, *Glauben und Verstehen* (Tübingen: Mohr, 1952), Vol. II, p. 232.
23 Ogden, *op. cit.*, p. 90.
24 *Ibid.*, p. 137.
25 *Ibid.*, p. 180.

man who chances to overhear theologians or believers talking to themselves or to each other?

Ronald Hepburn, a British linguistic analyst, has criticized Bultmann for evading the question of the validity of his claims. Verification and clarification are closely related, Hepburn has argued, and Bultmann has not made clear the logical structure of his theology. It is hidden behind the ambiguities and confusion in a number of his crucial terms and he has denied the validity of the empirical methods by which his claims could be verified.[26] Ogden's only answer is to point out that Hepburn has an inadequate understanding of Bultmann's specific use of the word "myth."[27] He fails to meet Hepburn's main point, which is that a translation of words does not change the facts to which the words refer.[28] If in the language of faith a statement about God is really a statement about man, if what faith speaks of is, "exhaustively and without remainder," man and his self-understanding, then to say that this is equally language about "God and his activities" is to assert that the same words refer to man, where they are verifiable, and to God, where they are not. That is confusing, to say the least. If "God loves me" means, "I feel secure, wanted, of value," then the second sentence can function perfectly well in place of the first. It does not follow, however, that "God loves me" will function in the place of "I feel secure." The statement, "I feel secure" is of the same sort as other statements about how we feel. We know what to do with this sort of statment. In its own way, it is subject to verification. We can observe, ask questions, put the speaker to the test, and at the end we can say, "Yes, that was the right word to use," or, "No, we don't ordinarily use the word 'secure' for such cases."[29] But the statement, "God loves me" has become notoriously im-

[26] R. Hepburn, "Demythologizing and the Problem of Validity," *New Essays*, pp. 227 ff.

[27] Ogden, *op. cit.*, p. 91 n.

[28] Hepburn, *op. cit.*, pp. 234 ff.

[29] Cf. Wittgenstein, *op. cit.*, §§ 247 ff., on the logical fallacy of a "private" language.

mune to any verification. Since the days of Elijah at Mt. Carmel, the statement has slowly died "the death of a thousand qualifications."[30] It refers to a being called "God," whether conceived as an elderly gentleman with a long beard, or masked in such mysterious and opaque words as "the ground and end of all things," just as surely as the statement, "I feel secure" refers to me and my attitude. Only one reference will not "stick" and the other will. One statement cannot be "cashed"; the other can. They are not the same, therefore, and if we insist on saying that one will function in place of the other and vice versa, then we have arrived at the place where muddle masquerades as mystery.

One wonders where the left wing existentialist theologians have found their "modern man." A man who shares the empirical spirit of our age cannot interchange these statements about God and man at all. For him, oblique language about God is no more useful than "objectifying" language about God. The problem lies in the word "God" itself, and in any other word supposedly referring to the "transcendent"; this is a problem to which we shall return in the next chapter.

3. This problem of words leads to our third objection: the kerygma of the New Testament contains statements which are empirical as well as some that are plainly existential, but its typical statements are mixed and their empirical aspect cannot logically be ignored. Bultmann says there are only two kinds of statements: those which offer objective information about the world or phenomena in it, and those which are existential, which call the hearer to a decision about his understanding of himself.[31] The former are simply empirical statements and are subject to verification in one way or another. Statements of faith and those of the kerygma are, according to Bultmann, entirely of the second type and they are not subject to proof. We would argue, however, that the New Testament proclamation contains primarily statements whose logic is at least partly empirical.

[30] Cf. Hepburn, *op. cit.*, p. 238.
[31] Cf. note 6, *supra*.

"The Word became flesh and dwelt among us" (John 1:14), for example, seems to be telling a fact, whatever other function it may have. "God was in Christ reconciling the world to himself" (II Cor. 5:19) sounds as if it were telling about a change in the situation of the world. "You have died, and your life is hid with Christ in God" (Col. 3:3) is telling us that our situation has been changed. Bultmann assures us, however, that the appearance of these statements is deceptive, and that the words they use are designed to pose a question for us about how we understand ourselves.

Bultmann contends that these words have to be understood as proclamation, as words spoken or written by those who would force us to face an existential question. That is perfectly true. These statements do urge the reader to answer a question about himself and his relation to the world; but they seem also to give information, suggesting an appropriate response to the state of affairs described. If a man crossing the ocean on a steamer rushes from his cabin shouting that the ship is on fire, he is certainly suggesting a course of action, however implicitly. The suggestion is to be taken seriously, however, only if the situation is as he has described it. A wise officer will begin by investigating to see if there is a fire, not by attempting to understand himself as a man who is on a burning ship. The language of the New Testament proclamation is logically of this sort. It proclaims that God has acted, that Jesus has been raised from the dead, that the powers of darkness have been overcome; in a word, that the situation of man has been changed. Something has happened, and the question of an appropriate response is obviously important. Paul proclaimed that God had reconciled the world to himself, and then he begged his readers to be reconciled to God (II Cor. 5:19–20). The importance of the appropriate response, either for those who heard the man shouting "Fire!" or for Paul's readers, is not a ground for simply ignoring the assertion of what has happened. As Paul pointed out, "If Christ has not been raised, then . . . your faith is in vain" (I Cor. 15:14). There are admittedly serious difficulties in taking the "ob-

jective" side of the Gospel as straightforward empirical assertions. Theologians of the existentialist left wing have seen that
if these assertions really are empirical, faith and the Gospel are
in trouble in the modern world, but the alternative of ignoring
these statements is no solution. As Hepburn has pointed out,
there are other alternatives to be considered, such as that of the
nonbeliever: that, in fact, faith is in vain. Our own alternative
will be reserved for the second half of this study, but in any case
the problem may not be avoided by focusing exclusively on the
existential side of the Gospel.

4. Our fourth objection to the position of the existentialist
"left" represented by Ogden is that (because of a lack of clarity
in the use of language and a failure to observe its logic) it dis-
places the historical event of Jesus of Nazareth by the existential
response of the believer. As readers of contemporary theology
know, the German language has two words for history. There is
Historie, which means the bare fact, the thing which happened.
There is also *Geschichte,* which means events together with their
significance. We have only one word in English, but we can
make distinctions and qualifications when we speak about past
events. If we mean a fact in the past, we can say so. If we mean
the significance or the importance of that fact (for its contemporaries, for us, or for both), we can also make that clear.

The need for this clarity may be seen in an assertion of
Ogden's which is typical of the position he represents: "The
New Testament speaks of the cross as 'the eschatological event,'
which never becomes an event in the past, but rather is con-
stantly present both in preaching and sacraments (cf. II Cor.
6:2; Rom. 6:3, 6; I Cor. 11:26) and in the believer's way of
conducting his life (II Cor. 4:10 f.; Gal. 5:24; 6:14; Phil.
3:10)."[32] One does not know whether to be more puzzled by the
strange use of words in this assertion or the fact that these texts
are cited to support it. In trying to understand his statement,

---

[32] Ogden, *op. cit.,* pp. 79 f.

we shall follow the suggestion of Anthony Flew, that "the meaning of [a word] can be elucidated by looking at simple paradigm cases: such as those in which fastidious language users employ [that word] when the madness of metaphysics is not upon them; such as those by reference to which the expression usually is, and ultimately has always to be, explained."[33] By any ordinary use of the verb "to speak," the New Testament does not speak of the cross as "the eschatological event." That is the language of the contemporary existentialist-theological position, not that of the authors of the New Testament. Whatever else may be said about the cross, it was two pieces of wood joined together and used for the execution of Jesus of Nazareth at a certain place and time, most definitely in the past. It cannot, for many obvious reasons, become present at all, least of all in words, unless the madness of metaphysics is truly upon us in considering this problem.

All sorts of things may be *added* to, but not substituted for, what we have just said. We can speak about the significance of the death of Jesus, about various ways in which that death has been or might be evaluated, but, unless we are to make a real *sacrificium intellectus* (when the intellect in question is informed by the empirical spirit of our times), the crucifixion of Jesus was at least an event of the distant past. It may or may not be a significant event which leads us to see ourselves and the world in a certain way, but it is an event of the past in any case. There is a serious problem in the language of those who propose an existentialist interpretation of the Gospel, and Ogden has led us even further away than Bultmann from what we ordinarily mean by history. Perhaps history is the *skandalon* of "the cross" for contemporary existentialists. In order to avoid this difficulty in our own restatement, we shall have to give a clear definition of history, one which requires no mental prestidigitation and which will enable us to do justice to the fact that

[33] A. Flew, "Divine Omnipotence and Human Freedom," *New Essays,* p. 150.

the New Testament proclaims that certain events, to which there were known witnesses, took place at certain times in the past.

As for Ogden's biblical citations, we must point out: (1) that although Paul says that "now is the day of salvation," he does not put his specific references to the death of Jesus in the present tense (II Cor. 5:14, 15, 21); (2) that the question of time and tense in Rom. 6:3 ff. is at least ambiguous; (3) that to proclaim an event does not involve the denial that that event has happened in the past; and (4) that the words "dead" and "crucified" are used of believers in a figurative way which differs from their literal use when referred to Jesus of Nazareth. One might say that the language of Paul is often poetic, but to deny that these passages refer to the death of Jesus as a specific event in the past is absurd. Of course more is said than merely that a certain man had died at a certain time, but not less.

5. Finally, we object that the proposal of the left wing, so compellingly stated by Ogden, circumvents Easter in defining the relationship of faith to Jesus of Nazareth. Bultmann, speaking as an historian, says that "what happened" on Easter was the inception of the faith of the disciples, which arose in connection with some sort of visionary experience.[34] He also implies that the decision of faith on Easter amounted to a renewal of the earlier decision of the disciples in Galilee to follow Jesus,[35] an implication which Ogden makes explicit: he asserts that Easter faith for the primitive Church *"was in reality its way of responding to the ministry of the historical Jesus."*[36] The issue had become sharper for the disciples as a result of Jesus' death, but the nature of faith, and that in which faith rested, remained unchanged. It is not surprising, therefore, that the resurrection

---

[34] Bultmann, *Kerygma und Mythos*, Vol. I, pp. 48 ff.; cf. Ogden, *op. cit.*, p. 87.

[35] Bultmann, *Theologie des Neuen Testaments*, Tübingen, J. C. B. Mohr, 1954, p. 45 f. (English translation by K. Grobel, *Theology of the New Testament*, New York, Scribner's, 1954, I, pp. 44 f.); cf. Ogden, *op. cit.*, p. 82.

[36] Ogden, *op. cit.*, p. 88.

plays no central part in his suggested solution of "Christ without myth." It is sufficient that what was always and everywhere man's possibility became concrete in the life of Jesus. The disciples responded to this with faith, which means that the possibility was actualized for them too. Other men in other times and places have also realized authentic existence, some quite apart from Jesus or the resurrection.[37] Feeling free to dispense with the resurrection and to understand faith apart from Easter, Ogden ends by dispensing with Jesus himself. This conclusion scarcely meets his own demand that any restatement of the Gospel should comprehend the major dimensions of that Gospel.

Ogden supports his contention that "the only final condition for sharing in authentic life that the New Testament lays down is a condition that can be formulated in complete abstraction from the event Jesus of Nazareth and all that it specifically imports,"[38] by a peculiar kind of exegesis. He claims that this assertion is "the clear and eloquent testimony" of (of all things!) the parable of the Last Judment in Matt. 25:31 ff. According to him, the point of the parable is that the only way to inherit the kingdom is to accept God's love and thus become free to respond to one's neighbor.[39] No mention is made of the fact, to which New Testament scholars call our attention, that close parallels to this parable exist in Egyptian and rabbinic sources, and that Jesus apparently was telling a story already well known in his time.[40] The significant fact is that Jesus changed one piece of the familiar story, and the "point" lies in this change, namely that the righteous do not know that they are righteous and the wicked do not know that they are wicked, a point which has nothing to do with Ogden's assertion.

We have made five objections to the alternative of the left

[37] *Ibid.*, p. 157.
[38] *Ibid.*, p. 143.
[39] *Ibid.*, pp. 143 f.
[40] J. Jeremias, *Die Gleichnisse Jesu* (6th ed., Göttingen, 1962): translated by S. H. Hooke, *The Parables of Jesus* (London: SCM Press, 1963), p. 208; J. Schniewind, *NTD, 2, Das Evangelium nach Matthäus* (Göttingen: Vandenhoeck & Ruprecht, 1950), p. 256.

wing position occupied by Ogden (and Bultmann) to the conservative interpretation of the Gospel. In our first three, we have said that even in its attempt to be "modern," it has not done justice to the secular, empirical spirit of our age. In our last two objections, we have argued that it has not done justice to the historical aspect of the Gospel.

An Analysis of the Radical Alternative

All we have said about the alternative of the "left" may be gathered together by analyzing the two theses in which Ogden summarizes Bultmann's program, Ogden's restatement of these theses, and his two principles for any valid restatement of the Gospel.

Bultmann's first thesis is that "Christian faith is to be interpreted exhaustively and without remainder as man's original possibility of authentic existence" as clarified by an existentialist analysis.[41] The word "original" cannot be meant empirically, for then it would refer to the first form of Homo sapiens, which does not appear to be what either Ogden or Bultmann has in mind. The word makes sense in this statement if it is taken as an indication of Bultmann's conviction that a man becomes his true (i.e. "original") self by becoming a believer. Ogden, by using the word "original" in the same way, apparently agrees. Taking "religion" in its most usual, everyday sense, then, we might say that Bultmann and Ogden are of the opinion that the most significant thing about a man is that he is (or is not) religious. "Believing," however, is nothing other and nothing more ("exhaustively and without remainder") than authentic existence as defined by Heidegger. To "exist authentically" is to be free from one's past and open to one's future. It is to be a true man, that which Bultmann and Ogden feel man should be.

41 Ogden, *op. cit.*, p. 112.

The final commitment of the left wing existential-theological position, therefore, is to the freedom of man as it has been defined by Heidegger. Heidegger is as essential to a theology resting on this thesis as Aristotle is to Thomism. For Ogden (and to some extent for Bultmann), the first thesis turns out to make a particular philosophy and its analysis of human existence into the final norm for faith.

The second thesis asserts that "Christian faith is actually realizable . . . only because of the event of Jesus of Nazareth. . . ."[42] The first thesis defines a norm to which Bultmann and Ogden are committed; the second has the appearance of being a statement of empirical causality, which it evidently is not. It is not a proposition based on a census of all who have ever been Christians, concluding that their authentic existence as free men was caused by the fact that there once was a man named Jesus. Of course, if there had never been such a man, there would never have been any "Christians," for "Christians" are those who have heard the story about Jesus and have generally thought that their conduct ought to have some sort of relationship to the things said about Jesus in the New Testament. (We have said this in an intentionally neutral way, as a statement in which believers and sceptics would both agree.) But is this historical precedence of Jesus the meaning of "only because"? Bultmann seems rather to say that faith is in fact a response to Jesus and his message, a response logically dependent on Jesus. If "faith" means the authentic existence of those who stand in a relationship to the message of Jesus, then the use of the restrictive word "only" is redundant but intelligible. This interpretation, however, is inconsistent with Bultmann's reluctance to assign a central role in his theology to historical fact. But if Bultmann really means that Jesus of Nazareth is essential to Christian faith, or to authentic existence, that presents a conflict with the first thesis. The only way in which to combine

<hr>

42 *Ibid.*

them is to say that Bultmann looks to two norms: Jesus and the New Testament on the one hand, and Heidegger on the other. Presumably the final arbiter is the Protestant theologian, or each believer for himself, and this is not a promising conclusion in a theology which offers to lead us out of the subjective snare of theological liberalism.

We have already noted that Ogden objects to this exclusiveness in Bultmann's second thesis, which makes for inconsistency in the program of demythologizing the Gospel and interpreting it existentially. For Ogden, who insists that all men are responsible for their existence, and that authentic existence must therefore always have been possible for all men, Bultmann's exclusiveness seems to deny human responsibility. Neither Ogden nor Bultmann, however, considers the logical necessity of any confession of faith containing an element of exclusiveness, insofar as it reflects the commitment of the believer to the object of his faith. If a man says that a certain situation in his life came about as a result of one thing only, and that the same change can happen to us only by the same agency, we should accept his declaration as meaning not that this is so, but that the man is thoroughly committed to that of which he is speaking. A man may offer us his grandmother's special cure for a throat infection, saying that it is the only thing which has helped him. That may or may not be the case, but it is probably true that he is convinced of it. If he says, moreover, that it will cure the sore throat of another man and that nothing else will, it is only a further indication of his conviction. If these statements are taken empirically, they are open to verification by experiment. As expressions of a conviction, however, they are also verifiable, for we should mistrust the man's assertion of conviction if he followed up his grandmother's formula with antibiotics. Taken either way, the statement is verifiable and therefore meaningful. There is no cause for confusion so long as the use is clear. But if the use is really to express a certain attitude or conviction, it is deceptive to dress up the statement as an empirical one.

Ogden, however, takes Bultmann's assertion of the dependence of faith on Jesus as an empirical statement. Since he fears that this assertion would deny the unqualified responsibility of man, he says "the ever-present ground and end of all created things" is the only prerequisite for faith. He qualifies this universal prerequisite, however, by saying that it is "decisively" manifested in Jesus of Nazareth, "fulfilling and correcting" all other manifestations of this "ground and end of all things." If this particular manifestation is that by which all the rest are judged ("decisive") and which makes up what is lacking in all the others ("fulfills and corrects"), it is the only complete and uncorrupted one. That is scarcely less restrictive than Bultmann's conclusion. This unsuccessful attempt to eliminate restrictive statements of faith arises from Ogden's failure to consider the logic of confessional statements.

Ogden lays down two principles for a constructive alternative to the theology of Bultmann. The first is that *"the demand for demythologizing that arises with necessity from the situation of modern man must be accepted without condition."*[43] The word "necessity" calls for analysis, for Ogden seems to feel that if Christians continued to preach the Gospel in its mythological form, "modern man" would not understand it; he would not see the real issue of the Gospel. According to the picture which Ogden seems to have in mind—the believer preaching and the unbelieving "modern man" listening—the "necessity" for demythologizing arises from the evangelistic task of the church. (Ogden takes for granted the necessity of evangelism.) Our picture, however, is of the Christian, himself a secular man, who realizes that the juxtaposition of his faith, expressed in traditional terms, and his ordinary way of thinking, causes a spiritual schizophrenia. The dilemma is hardly resolved by restricting his faith to only certain concerns, which he may call "spiritual," but which have no bearing on his life as a secular man. To rectify this situation he has the choice of forgetting about the Gospel and abandoning his faith or of finding a secular way in which to understand it. If he cannot forget the claim of the Gospel, then the "necessity" arises, not from some evangelistic task for the church, but from his desire to be a responsible and self-integrated Christian. He may admire or simply be puzzled by men who presume to know what the Gospel is and to translate it for him in the terms of his self-understanding, but their effort does not remove the "necessity" for him to work this out for himself. Ogden may also have a picture like ours in mind, as well as the more evident one of the evangelistic task, but we wish to be explicit about the nature of our picture. The question of the meaning of the Gospel for a secular empiricist who is seriously seeking to understand a faith which may be partly his own and partly inherited is prior to that of preaching to the modern unbeliever. Our secular Christian may well have made "a decision," but he is not at all clear what has thereby been decided. The "necessity" for understanding arises from his own situation, therefore, and not from that of anyone else, even though others may share his problem.

Ogden's second principle for constructing an alternative to Bultmann's proposal is that *"the sole norm of every legitimate theological assertion is the revealed word of God declared in Jesus Christ, expressed in Holy Scripture, and made concretely present in the proclamation of the church through its word and sacrament."*[44] For the "modern man" who is himself part of the present empirical era, this "norm" only begs the question. The man of our picture must conclude that Ogden is playing games with him, for it is just the meaning of such traditional terms as "the word of God" which poses the problem. What is Ogden's norm, this "word of God"? Since Ogden has said that when he talks about "God" he is actually talking about man, perhaps his "word of God" is really a human word, one that is "declared"

---

[44] *Ibid.,* p. 138.

in Jesus, "expressed" in the Bible, and "present" in the preaching of the church. If Ogden's variation on Bultmann's two theses conforms to this norm, this "word" is a self-understanding available to every man and conforming to Heidegger's analysis of existence. It is Heidegger who gives the final definition of Ogden's "norm."

The conclusion of the theological "left" leaves us with the difficulty of speaking about "transcendence," "ground and end of all things," or some other oblique phrase substituted for the word "God," which simply begs the empiricist's question. It leaves us with the center of the New Testament kerygma, Jesus the Messiah, displaced by an analysis of existence by a modern philosopher. Ogden protests against the christological interest of the conservative position and is convinced that the heart of the Gospel is represented by Theology rather than by Christology. But if the choice is between "God," however subtly hidden in oblique language, and the man Jesus of Nazareth, the empirically-minded, secular "believer" can only choose the latter, for he does not know what to do with Theology. Analogical as well as literal language about God makes no sense to him. He may or may not find existentialism's analysis of existence enlightening, but if he wishes to understand the Gospel, he cannot responsibly circumvent Jesus and the peculiar way in which his history is presented by the documents of the New Testament. Because the situation of "modern man" is in us and not outside of us, our analysis of the theological "left" as well as of the "right" leads us to reconsider the language of the New Testament concerning Jesus of Nazareth.

IV

ANALYSES OF

THEOLOGICAL LANGUAGE

The Problem of Religious Language

Many modern theologians say that one of the major difficulties confronting the Christian who is himself a secular man lies in the nature of religion and the confusion between religion and Christian faith. We have argued that the difficulty lies rather in the character of the language of faith, that the problem is not so much one of bad religion as it is one of bad, or at least unworkable, language. A discussion of the problem of religion and its language will introduce the third element of this study: the method of those who have reflected on the logical structures of various sorts of languages of faith.

Bultmann defines religion as the human longing to escape from this world, fed by the supposed discovery of "a sphere above this world, in which the soul alone, released from all that is worldly, could repose."[1] Such a longing and discovery would undoubtedly be called religious by most people, and a man who entertained such thoughts would be called a religious man, but

---

[1] In *Kerygma und Mythos,* Vol. I, pp. 26 f.

the concept of religion includes more than an other-worldly orientation. Many who undertake "religious activities," like going to church and singing hymns, or who say that certain events are according to "the will of God," do not show much interest in "a sphere above this world." Bultmann's definition meets only one aspect of the problem which concerns us.

Gerhard Ebeling, in an essay on Bonhoeffer's idea of religion, has given a more inclusive definition: the attempted "enlargement of reality by means of God."[2] Religion consists of appealing to God as a means of explaining, justifying, or otherwise "filling in the picture" of the world or human affairs. This summarizes the characteristics of religion, as Bonhoeffer saw them: thinking of two spheres of reality, the natural and the supernatural; interest in the other-worldly; metaphysical thinking; an idea of transcendence which surpasses human possibilities.[3] The religionless posture, on the other hand, is that of "coming to terms with reality apart from God," or without use of the God-hypothesis.[4]

Contemporary theologians from Barth to Ogden are agreed that Christianity does not conform to this definition of religion. Religion, they would say, is man's use of God to solve some human problem, whereas the Gospel proclaims God's unexpected use of man for his own purposes; this distinction lies behind Bonhoeffer's search for a "nonreligious" interpretation of biblical concepts. The fact remains, however, that all of these theologians continue to speak of God, even though, as Ebeling put it, "a considerable proportion of our contemporaries haven't the least idea of what we are even talking about when we speak of God."[5] Ebeling himself proposes what he calls a "worldly" way to speak of God, a way which must be concrete, clear, and effective, but the same "considerable proportion of our contem-

2 G. Ebeling, *Wort und Glaube* (Tübingen: Mohr, 1960), p. 145.

3 Bonhoeffer, *Ethics*, trans. N. H. Smith (London: SCM Press, 1955), p. 62; *WE*, pp. 180, 182, 184, 241 f., 259 f.

4 Ebeling, *op. cit.*, p. 159.

5 *Ibid.*, p. 363.

poraries" would undoubtedly judge this way to be talk about God nevertheless. Ebeling sees the problem, but he has not solved it.

The solution proposed by existentialist theologians consists of eliminating all "objectification" of God in thought and word,[6] but since Bultmann also objects to using the word "God" simply as a symbol for human experience, the word "God" appears to refer to nothing at all. The "nonobjective" use of the word "God" allows of no verification and is therefore meaningless. The moment we begin to use the word in a qualified sense, as in Flew's parable, we begin to kill our assertions by the "death of a thousand qualifications," and we end by making no assertion at all.[7] We do not understand, therefore, by what logic Bultmann and Ebeling continue to use the word "God" as though it had a quite specific reference. The *we* must be emphasized and explained. Why do we not understand their use of the word "God" as though it had a quite specific reference? Such a use does appear to conflict with their confessed existentialist concerns and is therefore unclear, but our chief difficulty lies elsewhere. We set out upon this study with certain acknowledged commitments to what we called "secular thought," and we said that secularism, as we were using the term, is grounded in empirical attitudes in some way. Our objection to a certain use of the word "God" says as much about our own empirical attitudes as it does about Bultmann and Ebeling. The nature and extent of these empirical attitudes will become clearer as the study develops. It can only be suggested, not proved, that these attitudes are more common among contemporary "believers" than Bultmann or Ebeling appear to recognize, the force of this suggestion being measured by the degree to which a method

---

[6] Cf., for example, E. Fuchs, "Glaube und Geschichte im Blick auf die Frage nach dem historischen Jesus," *Zeitschrift für Theologie und Kirche*, 54.2, 1957; also the discussion in Chapter III, *supra*.

[7] Cf. T. R. Miles, *Religion and the Scientific Outlook*, pp. 147 ff., on the meaninglessness of "qualified literal theism," a faith expressed by Flew's believing explorer.

consistent with such attitudes is found to be helpful for the reader.

The contemporary theological fashion of setting the Christian Gospel over against "religion" does not clarify our problem.[8] According to this view of the matter, the Gospel proclaims God's act of grace reaching down to rescue man, whereas religion has to do with man reaching up to find or define God. The "religionless" man, however, who can come to terms with life quite apart from this literally nonsensical entity called "God," will not be impressed by the difference between the Gospel and "religion." There is a difference between them, but both the Gospel and "religion" have so much more in common than either has with the scepticism of a man like Flew that the distinction loses its interest. The empiricist in us finds the heart of the difficulty not in what is said about God, but in the very talking about God at all. We do not know "what" God is, and we cannot understand how the word "God" is being used. It seems to function as a name, yet theologians tell us that we cannot use it as we do other names, to refer to something quite specific. If it is meant to refer to an "existential encounter," a point of view, or the speaker's self-understanding, surely a more appropriate expression could be found. The problem is not solved, moreover, by substituting other words for the word *God:* one could supply the letter X (Flew used the word *gardener* in his parable) and the problem would remain, for the difficulty has to do with how X functions. The problem of the Gospel in a secular age is a problem of the logic of its apparently meaningless language, and linguistic analysts will give us help in clarifying it. We dare to call *our* problem *the* problem not because we have access to what everyone or anyone else means by "secular age" or "Gospel," but because we dare to hope that what we have found helpful for our own understand-

---

[8] Bonhoeffer, who approved of this fashion, gave Barth credit for being one of its main champions. *WE*, p. 219.

ing may prove helpful for others, who may then identify the
problem to some extent as we have identified it.

Linguistic Analyses of Religious Assertions

Flew's parable, with which we began our study, has been
answered by R. M. Hare,[9] who begins by granting that Flew is
"completely victorious" on the grounds which he has marked
out. Hare grants that if religious or theological assertions are
taken as statements about "how things are" (this is indeed the
form they seem to have: *e.g.* "God loves all men"; "Jesus Christ
is Lord"; "the wages of sin is death"), they must be judged as
meaningless. The logic of Flew's parable is perfectly sound.
Having made this concession, Hare has cleared the way for his
reply. He begins by telling another parable about a student who
has a peculiar attitude about dons: he is convinced that they all
want to kill him. However many apparently friendly dons he
meets, however friends try to persuade him by recalling his
own experience or theirs, his attitude does not change.

Hare has invented the word *blik* for a fundamental attitude.
The student in his parable has an insane "blik" about dons; we
have a sane one, we would say, for Hare points out that we are
never without a "blik," or we could not say that the student is
insane, that he is wrong and we are right. A "blik" is not
achieved by empirical inquiry. The basic presuppositions we
have about the world are not verifiable, and yet everything we
do depends on them, as Hume taught us. Such a presupposition
or set of presuppositions (and all men have them) are not to be
regarded as *explanations*. That is Flew's mistake; he took his
Believer's "blik" to be an explanation of the clearing in the
jungle, which it clearly is not. Hare points out that "bliks" are
serious matters for those who hold them, whether we judge any

[9] *New Essays*, pp. 99-105.

particular "blik" to be right or wrong, and everyone has a "blik." Consequently, the detachment of Flew's two explorers is unreal.

Flew's response to Hare's suggestion focuses nicely on our problem:[10]

> Any attempt to analyse Christian religious utterances as expressions or affirmations of a *blik* rather than as (at least would-be) assertions about the cosmos is fundamentally misguided. *First,* because thus interpreted they would be entirely unorthodox. If Hare's religion really is a *blik,* involving no cosmological assertions about the nature and activities of a supposed personal creator, then surely he is not a Christian at all? *Second,* because thus interpreted, they would scarcely do the job they do. If they were not even intended as assertions then many religious activities would become fraudulent, or merely silly. If 'You ought *because* it is God's will' asserts no more than 'You ought,' then the person who prefers the former phraseology is not really giving a reason, but a fraudulent substitute for one, a dialectical dud cheque.

The issue between these two philosophers does not concern the logic or function of language. Neither of them, moreover, has questioned the empirical picture of the world of the twentieth century. Both grant that a simple literal theism, whose assertions could be put to an empirical test like that of Elijah before Mt. Carmel, is untenable. In other words, they agree in denying an "objectified" God. They also agree, however, that if a simple literal theism is untenable, a qualified literal ("nonobjectified") theism is meaningless. It is dead by the death of a thousand qualifications. If God is really "wholly other," we cannot speak of him at all. If statements about God are "to be interpreted exhaustively and without remainder" as statements about man, they cannot be meaningful statements about God. Where these philosophers disagree is on the nature of Christianity. One calls

[10] *Ibid.,* pp. 107-08.

the statements of faith a collection of cosmological assertions; the other sees them as expressions of a "blik," an orientation, a commitment to see the world in a certain way, and a way of life following inevitably upon this orientation. What Hare is suggesting is that a man's faith and his theology have a meaning, even though the theistic rug has been pulled out from under him.

Not all analysts of the language of faith have gone this far, but Ian T. Ramsey, in arguing for the meaningfulness of language about God, offers support for and further elaboration of Hare's concept of a "blik." He argues that the language of faith combines the language of discernment, of an admittedly special sort, with the language of commitment, of a sort which covers the totality of life and the world.[11] Statements of faith direct our attention to certain kinds of situations: situations of disclosure, when "the light dawns," and the situation becomes alive and new. The emphasis is not only on the disclosure or discernment, but also on the resulting commitment, whereby what we now "see" becomes important and determines our subsequent seeing. In such situations, the believer makes use of odd words like "God."

The function of such words is clarified with the help of Ramsey's idea of models and qualifiers. The model of "father," for example, points in a certain direction, inviting us to follow this direction. But it is qualified by such words as "eternal" or "omnipotent," to indicate that the word is only a model, that we should push on and on and on . . . until the light dawns, and the situation, and, with it, all things, takes on "depth," or rather, until we see that the "depth" is there to be discerned. Ramsey grants that all this sounds very close to a psychological explanation of religious language, but he argues that it is false to say that such an interpretation of human experience is "purely sub-

[11] *Religious Language,* pp. 18 ff.

jective," since there is in fact no such thing as a purely subjective experience. Every experience is an experience of something.

The language of faith is nothing if not odd, Ramsey says, and he stresses its peculiarity in order to counter two "popular misconceptions: that those with an intense affection for ordinary language must necessarily deny metaphysics," and "that those who defend metaphysics must necessarily trade in occult realms and shadowy worlds."[12] One example of the odd character of the language of faith is the name of God, which the Hebrews avoided whenever possible. The significance of this avoidance of God's name lies in the linguistic fact that discovering a name is typical of situations of disclosure or discernment. When we *assign* a name to something, no disclosure is involved; we are simply in the realm of external information. When someone tells us his name, however, or when we learn a name, the situation is a religious one, involving mystery and eliciting awe. The use of the revealed name recalls the mystery of self-disclosure.[13] The text of the revelation of the divine name in chapter 3 of Exodus is, moreover, an example of the final form of the language of loyalty. The last answer to why I have acted as I have, after all the partial explanations, is the statement, "I'm I." Behind any other things I might say, like "because I decided to do it," or "because he asked me to do it," lies this ultimate causal explanation. The series of "whys" of any decision, any case of loyalty or commitment, must finally come to rest at the "logical stop-card": "I'm I."[14] The word "God" also, Ramsey says, functions as the tautology "I'm I," and it is just this statement, "I am who I am," which stands in place of the revealed name in chapter 3 of Exodus. This tautology marks the limit which religious language approaches and to which it tries to point. The limit is never part of the series of variables which

[12] I. T. Ramsey, *Freedom and Immortality* (London: SCM Press, 1960), p. 152.
[13] *Religious Language*, pp. 108 ff.
[14] *Ibid.*, pp. 63 ff.

approach that limit, yet there is a relationship between the variables and the limit.[15]

Another example of the oddness of biblical language is the story of the resurrection of Jesus. The question "Did the resurrection occur?" is misleadingly simple, for if "resurrection" referred only to such things as an empty tomb and a resuscitated body, then one could acknowledge the resurrection and yet not be a believer. What the Christian believes about the resurrection of Jesus has something to do with these observable factors, but it is not identical with them. In fact, the question "Did the resurrection occur?" is logically much more like the question asked of a situation in which a man has jumped from a bridge to rescue a drowning child: "Was that a case of duty?" The empirical evidence is not irrelevant, but the evidence will never settle either question. The word "resurrection" (like the words "duty," "love," and "God") directs us to the sort of situation in which a discernment fundamental to our whole conception of life and a response of commitment may take place. Such situations exceed empirical description, however relevant description may be to our discernment.

A further illustration of Ramsey's analysis of the language

[15] At several places, Ramsey touches on a point which has been of concern to William Poteat: the possibility of understanding the function of theological language in the light of the similarly strange use of the word "I." (William Poteat, " 'I Will Die': An Analysis," *Philosophical Quarterly*, Vol. IX, No. 34 [1959], pp. 3-15.) Poteat has urged reflection upon the way in which "I" functions when we say, "I was born," or "I will die," where it operates in a way quite different from that of the word "he" when we say, "He was born," or "He will die." "He" functions in a straightforwardly empirical manner. We can say, "He will die," and also, after the fact, "He died." But we cannot use the first person singular of the verb "to die" in the past, unless we have first changed radically the manner of using the word "die." This indicates something odd about the logic of the verbs "to die" and "to be born," but more important, it indicates the odd logic of the first person singular pronoun. Of course, I can say many things about myself which are empirical and can also be said of me by someone else. But there are also other things which only I can say about myself and which cannot be translated "exhaustively and without remainder" into what others may say about me. This line of reflection is related to the distinction which existentialists make between the words "existential" and "existentialist." The first has to do with the "I"; the second can be talked about equally well in the third person.

of faith may be seen in his treatment of the language of classical Christology:

> For the Early Christians, Jesus Christ was the occasion of and the object of "disclosure" situations for which the word "God" would have been appropriate currency. Further, much could be said about Jesus Christ which was, on the face of it, straightforwardly empirical, viz. that he was tired, that he wept, and so on. So we have what are *prima facie,* two logically different languages competing as descriptions of the object of "disclosure" or "revelation." There then arises the problem of how these two languages can somehow be integrated, for in the Christian disclosure *only one* "object" is disclosed.
>
> Hence arises the concept of "hypostatic" unity, which we may interpret both from a linguistic and a "factual" point of view.
>
> (i) To know what hypostatic unity is *in fact,* there must be evoked a Christian disclosure situation with Jesus Christ as the occasion and object of it.[16]

Preaching and the celebration of the Lord's Supper are obviously intended to evoke such a situation. The object and occasion of disclosure is the man Jesus, and the disclosure comes (if it does come) when "the light dawns" and we find ourselves involved in what existentialists would call an "encounter." All sorts of models may help us toward this situation, but none can either produce or describe it. Ramsey's analysis continues:

> (ii) As far as *language* goes, . . . the doctrine of *communicatio idiomatum* (the participation of either "nature" of Christ in the properties or attributes of the other) and the word "hypostasis" may both be seen as an ancient attempt to deal with what nowadays would be called the problem of complementary languages and their unity, a problem which is raised especially by recent developments in scientific method. Let me emphasize that hypostasis would only be success-

16 *Religious Language,* pp. 166 f.

ful in unifying two languages if it is odd enough never to be given except by reference to a Christian disclosure situation. If it is to be the logical bond that Christian doctrine wishes it to be, it cannot be modelled. If it is to do this work it is quite impossible (*logically* impossible) to produce a model for it.[17]

We have quoted Ramsey at length because this passage is one of the rare examples of the beginning of an analysis of the language of Christology. Moreover, Ramsey has made in effect a further development of Hare's concept of "blik." A "blik" involves a perspective entailing a commitment, and Ramsey has clarified this with his analysis of the language of discernment and commitment. When this analysis is applied to the language of Christology, it discloses two sorts of languages: one is the language of a "blik"; the other is that of straightforward empirical observation. Both sorts of language are used about the same person, Jesus of Nazareth. But the language of Christology is appropriate only to one who himself has discerned what Christians discern, for whom Jesus has become the occasion for a new discernment which has led to a commitment involving his whole perspective. We can summarize by saying that the language of Christology is language about Jesus of Nazareth on the part of those for whom he has been the occasion and remains the definition of their "blik."

Another analysis of the language of faith, similar to those of Hare and Ramsey, has been made by T. R. Miles. Accepting, as Hare has done, the argument of Flew, Miles recommends what he calls "the way of silence qualified by parables." In place of the language of "simple literal theism" (God walking in the garden of Eden, coming down to and scattering the builders of the tower of Babel, smelling Noah's sacrifice), which few men would use today, and the language of "qualified literal theism" (the language of the Believer in Flew's parable), which

17 *Ibid.,* pp. 168 f.

proves to have no "cash value," Miles urges the course of silence, in which no claims or assertions are made. The Believer may qualify his silence, however, by what Miles calls the theistic parable.[18]

Any parable has three characteristics: the question of the literal truth of the parable is unimportant, the language is straightforwardly empirical, and, most important, the parable has a message. It invites us to view in a certain way the situation in connection with which the parable is told. Empirical considerations may be relevant for deciding on the usefulness of a particular parable, however. If, for example, it could be proved historically that Jesus "was fallible on matters of importance, it would be all the more difficult to accept any parable which says that he is the incarnate son of God."[19] Ultimately, however, the choice of parables is a matter of "personal conviction rather than rational argument."[20] The believer is the man who has chosen to qualify his silence with the theistic parable, like the one expressed in the doctrine of the creation of the world by a loving Father. The question of whether the parable is "objectively true" can only be met by silence; but the whole outlook of the man who chooses the theistic parable is changed.

One of the most radical contributions to the analysis of the language of faith has been made by R. B. Braithwaite. We shall summarize his lectures[21] because his argument is important for our study. Braithwaite begins by applying the verification principle of modern philosophy in its sharpest form to the language of the Christian faith. This principle implies

that the primary question becomes, not whether a religious statement such as that a personal God created the world is true or false, but how it could be known to be true or false.

[18] Miles, op. cit., pp. 161 ff.
[19] Ibid., p. 172.
[20] Ibid., p. 171.
[21] An Empiricist's View of Religious Belief (Cambridge: Cambridge University Press, 1955).

Unless this latter question can be answered, the religious statement has no ascertainable meaning and there is nothing expressed by it to be either true or false. Moreover a religious statement cannot be believed without being understood, and it can only be understood by an understanding of the circumstances which would verify or falsify it. Meaning is not logically prior to the possibility of verification: we do not first learn the meaning of a statement, and afterwards consider what would make us call it true or false; the two understandings are one and indivisible.[22]

Now "a hypothesis which is consistent with every possible empirical fact is not an empirical one." Unless an answer can be given as to how the world or the course of history would have been different without God, or unless it were admitted that if either had been different we could have concluded that there is no God, religious or theological propositions cannot be empirical.[23] In short, if Elijah's empirical test is no longer to be allowed, then neither are assertions that Elijah's God has acted empirically in this world!

Braithwaite then states his thesis: religious assertions are in fact *used as* moral assertions.[24] Moral assertions share with religious ones the characteristic of being neither logically necessary nor empirical; yet they have a use: that of guiding conduct. With the significant modification which has been made in the early verification principle (so that philosophers would now say that "the meaning of a statement is given by the way in which it is used"),[25] it is now realized that "the primary use of a moral assertion [is] that of expressing the intention of the asserter to act in a particular sort of way specified in the assertion."[26]

---

[22] Braithwaite, *op. cit.*, pp. 2, 3.
[23] *Ibid.*, pp. 6, 7.
[24] *Ibid.*, p. 11.
[25] *Ibid.*, p. 10. Braithwaite refers to Wittgenstein, *op. cit.*, §§ 340, 352, 559 f. Cf. note 22, Chapter I, *supra.*
[26] *Ibid.*, p. 12.

Braithwaite then returns to his thesis that religious assertions are "primarily declarations of adherence to a policy of action, declarations of commitment to a way of life," and continues his argument:

> That the way of life led by the believer is highly relevant to the sincerity of his religious convictions has been insisted upon . . . by Christianity. . . . The view which I put forward for your consideration is that the intention of a Christian to follow a Christian way of life is not only the criterion for the sincerity of his belief in the assertions of Christianity; it is the criterion for the meaningfulness of his assertions. Just as the meaning of a moral assertion is given by its use in expressing the asserter's intention to act, so far as in him lies, in accordance with the moral principle involved, so the meaning of a religious assertion is given by its use in expressing the asserter's intention to follow a specified policy of behaviour. To say that it is belief in the dogmas of religion which is the cause of the believer's intending to behave as he does is to put the cart before the horse: it is the intention to behave which constitutes what is known as religious conviction.[27]

Braithwaite is aware of two objections which might be raised here: not all theological assertions imply action; and, there is a difference between religion and morality. He meets these objections, first, by admitting that religious assertions should be taken as a group and in context. He insists, however, that "unless a Christian's assertion that God is love (*agape*)—which I take to epitomize the assertions of the Christian religion—be taken to declare his intention to follow an agapeistic way of life, he could be asked what is the connection between the assertion and the intention, between Christian belief and Christian practice."[28] (This would presumably be Braithwaite's exegesis of I John 4:20: "If any one says, 'I love God,' and hates his brother, he is

27 *Ibid.*, pp. 15 f.
28 *Ibid.*, p. 18.

a liar.") Second, he also grants that being filled with *agape* is more than acting agapeistically: "it also includes an agapeistic frame of mind."[29] But more important, for Braithwaite, is the following distinction: "A religious assertion will . . . have a propositional element which is lacking in a purely moral assertion, in that it will refer to a story as well as to an intention." Consequently, "to assert the whole set of assertions of the Christian religion is both to tell the Christian doctrinal story and to confess allegiance to the Christian way of life."[30] He notes that what he calls "story" has also been called by other names: parable, fairy tale, allegory, fable, tale, and myth. He prefers the word "story" because it is neutral, "implying neither that the story is believed nor that it is disbelieved."[31] The Christian story includes straight history and also material clearly not historical. But Braithwaite insists that belief in the empirical truth of the stories "is not the proper criterion for deciding whether or not an assertion is a Christian one. A man is not, I think, a professing Christian unless he both proposes to live according to Christian moral principles and associates his intention with thinking of Christian stories; but he need not believe that the empirical propositions presented by the stories correspond to empirical fact."[32]

What is the function of these stories and how are they related to this intention to act? Braithwaite answers that the stories have a psychological and causal relationship to the intention: to say that an action is "doing the will of God" helps us to carry it through, and Braithwaite feels that theologians need to keep in

---

[29] *Ibid.*, p. 21.

[30] *Ibid.*, p. 24: "Entertainment in thought (of a part or the whole of the Christian story) forms the context in which Christian resolutions are made, which serves to distinguish Christian assertions from those made by adherents of another religion or of no religion." We would urge the reader, who may feel that this is insufficient and that there must be something distinctively "Christian" about the actions or words themselves of believers, to reflect on the motives of such feelings.

[31] *Ibid.*, p. 26.

[32] *Ibid.*, pp. 26 f. The word "principles" in this context means "assertions" or "convictions."

mind the psychological fact that men's behaviour is determined not only by intellectual considerations, but also by phantasies, imaginations, and hopes.[33] He concludes his essay by remarking that in his analysis of theological language, he has not come across an entity called belief. "Religious belief," he concludes, is not "a species of ordinary belief, of belief in propositions. A moral belief is an intention to behave in a certain way: a religious belief is an intention to behave in a certain way (a moral belief) together with the entertainment of certain stories associated with the intention in the mind of the believer."[34]

If there is a weak link in this chain of reasoning, it is Braithwaite's understanding of the function of the Christian "story" and its relationship to the intention to lead the Christian "way of life." While his psychological observation is in order, his solution does not do justice to the indispensable role of the "story" in the kerygma. We shall return to a further analysis of this role in our reconstruction. The position of Braithwaite is, however, sufficiently close to the others we have examined to allow us to speak of a rough consensus among contemporary analysts of the language of faith, in spite of the variety of thought within that consensus.

Not all analytic philosophers, of course, have approached the language of faith in the way we have presented. A number of philosophers have argued that faith is a kind of knowledge and that faith-statements are to be understood cognitively, somewhat as Flew understands them. They would take issue with Hare, Braithwaite, and Miles, among others, insisting that faith is logically "belief that . . ." before it is "belief in. . . ." Christianity, they argue, is not essentially a conviction, commitment, or attitude, but entry into and living in a relationship with a transcendent being, and it stands or falls with the meaningfulness of its assertions concerning that transcendent being. Passing over the difficulties arising from placing the word "relationship"

---

[33] *Ibid.*, pp. 27, 28, 31.
[34] *Ibid.*, pp. 32 f.

alongside of the expression "transcendent being," we notice a common line of argument among several philosophers holding this position.[35] Fundamental to their case is the concept of undifferentiated or natural theism. Arguing from a sense of contingency, or from some other variation of the argument from design, they believe that most men, or a number great enough to lead us to take note of their ideas, have at least some vague concept of that which is *not* contingent and to which the designation "divine" would seem to them to be appropriate. On the basis of this general concept of the divine, certain events are interpreted by religious men as manifesting in some way and to some degree the character, will, or activity of this transcendent being. In some forms of this argument, a strong appeal is made to Jesus as the authority for looking to certain particular events and interpreting them as revelations of the divine. In the last resort, those who take this approach to the language of faith grant that verification must apply to this language, but they argue that this can only be done in the *eschaton,* in the final day of the Kingdom. In the *eschaton,* we shall see clearly whether or not faith as knowledge is correct. If that is no proof for the present, it is at least a justification for saying that faith-statements are meaningful, even though we cannot yet be in the position to carry through this verification. Logically, however, the statements of faith are in principle verifiable, and therefore meaningful, as cognitive assertions.

The choice of a noncognitive, "blik" conception of faith, rather than of a cognitive conception, will be fundamental to our study. We make this choice for both logical and theological reasons. The cognitive approach requires speaking of that which it admits is ineffable. It involves speaking of God by analogy, yet it is granted by its proponents that they cannot say

[35] Representative of this position are I. M. Crombie, "The Possibility of Theological Statements," *Faith and Logic,* pp. 31 ff., and John Hick, *Faith and Knowledge* (Ithaca, N. Y.: Cornell University Press, 1957); "Theology and Verification," *Theology Today,* Vol. XVII, No. 1 (1960), pp. 12 ff.

to what extent the analogies are apt and proper. More difficult, however, is the problem of an appeal to eschatological verification. If "in heaven" there is neither marriage nor giving in marriage, then it is at least questionable if there is what philosophers call "verification" in the *eschaton*. On what basis could the possibility of eschatological verification be affirmed or denied? The language in which this question must be settled is, for better or worse, the language of men, not the "language of angels." To speak of verification as philosophers do presupposes certain empirical attitudes, and no one knows the empirical attitudes which would be either possible in or appropriate to the *eschaton*.

We reject the cognitive approach to theological language, however, not primarily because it is logically puzzling, but because of certain theological commitments out of which this study has arisen. That approach builds its case on a natural sense of the divine, on natural religion and a natural revelation. The history of theology, seen from the perspective of modern kerygmatic theology, suggests that this is a road leading into the wilderness. Within the Protestant tradition, that road has been clearly charted and firmly marked with a "dead-end" sign by the work of Karl Barth, and we see no reason to ignore the warning. Christian faith has troubles enough in the twentieth century without retracing the misleading path opened up for Protestantism by the rationalist orthodoxy of the seventeenth century, followed to its unproductive end in the nineteenth century.

The cognitive approach to faith-statements presented by some linguistic analysts leads into the old inner contradiction of earlier forms of natural theology. It begins by speaking of a divine being of whom it *cannot* be said that this is the God of grace, the God who finds man wandering into idolatry with every conception he forms of the divine, the God who comes and makes himself known to man, not through, but in spite of, man's natural conceptions of the divine. Either the "God" of which Christians have tried to speak is the God of grace and *self*-revelation, or he is the neutral "it" of natural theology. The "divine being" of the cognitive approach is not easily assimilable to Pascal's " *'Dieu d'Abraham, Dieu d'Isaac, Dieu de Jacob,' non des philosophes et des savants.*"

To follow the cognitive approach to religious language would contradict our point of departure. It tends to mark off a certain area of experience as "religious," and it argues for a religious way of knowing, in contrast to other (secular?) ways of knowing. This approach leads Christians into the trap of the reductionist tendency of nineteenth-century theology, where they are tempted to fight a defensive action against all other knowledge in order to defend some small area of their own which they may call the proper sphere of theology, concerning which they may cry—but surely cry in vain—that nonreligious knowledge should not try to tread on this holy ground. On the basis of these logical and theological objections, we judge the cognitive approach to theological language to be inadequate to the character of secular thought and to the heart of the Gospel.

We cannot argue, of course, for some objective, normative definition of verification or of the Gospel. When we call this approach inadequate, we are exposing our own categorial commitments which we see reflected in some modern kerygmatic theology, some modern analytic philosophy, and indicated with the word "secular." We can only acknowledge that our commitments are such as to lead us to reject a search for a religious preserve to be investigated by a special religious way of knowing, and we are committed to a Gospel which begins, not with an argument for undifferentiated theism, but with the impact of whatever it was that happened on Easter in the context of a particular history. With such commitments, we have no choice but to return to the consensus of such analysts as Hare and Braithwaite about the character of the language of faith and to assess its possibilities as a tool for determining what we have called the secular meaning of the Gospel.

The first point of consensus is that "simple literal theism" is wrong and that "qualified literal theism" is meaningless. The second agreement lies in the implicit or explicit conviction that the language of faith does have a meaning, and that this meaning can be explored and clarified by linguistic analysis. The third consensus is a concern to take Christianity seriously as a way of life, even though a straightforward use of the word "God" must be abandoned.

Simple literal theism is wrong and qualified literal theism is meaningless. The first of these assertions is another way of making Bultmann's point that myth is no longer tenable; the idea of the empirical intervention of a supernatural "God" in the world of men has been ruled out by the influence of modern science on our thinking. In making such statements, we reveal our own commitments to modern science, and we would only add that modern thought tends to grant the validity of the findings of the natural sciences. For those holding these commitments, thunderbolts can no longer be explained as weapons of the wrath of an invisible God, and the phrase "God did this," therefore, cannot logically mean what it says.[36] If we begin to qualify this phrase, however, we find one qualification calling for another until nothing is left of the original assertion. Linguistic analysis challenges the qualified theism of Bultmann and Ogden as much as that of more conservative theologians. Whether objectifying or nonobjectifying, language about a "God who acts" must be interpreted in some other way.

The language of faith has a meaning, nonetheless; it has a function which may be clarified by linguistic analysis. The language of Christian faith is the language of a believer, one who has been "caught" by the Gospel. In so far as his "blik" is functioning, his language is the language of faith, whether he is speaking about some generally recognized religious subject, such as "God," or of some so-called secular subject, like politics or his job. The function of his words may be to enlighten his

---

[36] For a similar criticism of such assertions of biblical theology as "God acts" and "God speaks," cf. Langdon B. Gilkey, "Cosmology, Ontology, and the Travail of Biblical Language," *The Journal of Religion*, Vol. XLI, No. 3 (1961), pp. 194 ff.

listener concerning his "blik." In other circumstances they may take the form of an invitation to share that "blik." Or they may simply be a notification that he must take a particular course of action, for the unexpressed reason that he sees things in a certain way. In each case, the fact that a believer is speaking and the circumstances in which he is speaking may not be ignored. The actual function of the words is the key to understanding the language of faith.

Finally, the language of faith has meaning when it is taken to refer to the Christian way of life; it is not a set of cosmological assertions. The Christian "way of life," an expression recalling the New Testament designation of life in Christ as "the Way" (Acts 9:2), is central to the linguistic interpretation we have been considering. It contains elements of wonder, awe, and worship, but it is bound up with a basic conviction concerning the world and man's place in it which bears directly on decisions and actions. There is a parallel to the existentialists' emphasis on decision, but room is left for attitudes and ways of seeing things for which we would not ordinarily use the word "decision." There is a note of British calm and logical reflection in this conception of what goes to make up the Christian "way of life" or "authentic existence." Yet for these thinkers also, a "blik," the discernment and commitment of faith, is by definition something which is "lived."

This attempt to define a consensus does justice to no single position of the language analysts, yet our summary indicates the trend of their interpretations of Christianity. It remains to evaluate the method and results of these philosophers for a reconstruction of the kerygma and Christology.

A Method for Reconstruction

From Flew's parable through Braithwaite's argument, the analyses of theological language constitute a clarification which shows us where problems may be dissolved and where the real problems of the language of faith lie. This clarification has been accomplished by a frankly empirical method which reflects the thinking of an industrialized, scientific age. It has taken certain empirical attitudes characteristic of modern thought seriously and accepted them without qualification. In the frank recognition that the lot of oblique language about God is no better, and in some ways worse, than that of simple literal theism, we come face to face with our real problem of understanding the Gospel today: the difficulty of finding any meaningful way to speak of God. We can no longer share the faith of the man who thought that his god lived in a tree and that his god would die if the tree were burned down, or who conceded the weakness of a god who did not respond to calls for help from the dangers of nature or man. We should say he was mistaken, but his religious assertions were understandable. An assertion of qualified literal theism, on the other hand, is meaningless, and the moral exasperation of Flew's sceptical explorer is not to be dismissed lightly by those who claim to serve the truth. Miles's suggestion of silence is very much in order at this point, and if theology at its best has not meant to infringe on this silence, its reticence has not always been obvious.

These analyses of theological language express with clarity and force the unity of ethics and theology. Contemporary theology has said that Christian ethics is dependent on theology; these philosophers say that theology may not be independent of ethics. They have acknowledged, of course in their own way, the warning against saying "Lord, Lord" (Luke 6:46), or "The Temple of the Lord! The Temple of the Lord!" (Jer. 7:4). They even emphasize the empirical, human, historical, and ethical side of the Gospel at the expense of its divine, cosmological, trans-historical, and supernatural elements. Christologically speaking, these interpretations imply holding to the humanity of Christ, to the man Jesus of Nazareth, and letting the issue of his divinity fall where it may.

Our last statement is an exaggeration, but it reminds us of

the question raised by Flew in his response to Hare's suggestion of "blik": what is the real issue in Christian faith: Jesus or God, Christology or Theology? The linguistic analysts we have considered, especially Hare and Braithwaite, tend to choose the former, in contrast to Ogden. Flew raises the question of orthodoxy, but what is orthodoxy in this era when many sincere Christians do not know what to do with the word "God" or can use it only in a way entirely different from the "orthodox" way of the early centuries of Christianity? Today, we cannot even understand the Nietzschian cry that "God is dead!" for if it were so, how could we know? No, the problem now is that the *word* "God" is dead.

A loose way of characterizing these analyses of the language of faith is to say that "God-statements" have been translated into "man-statements." (This is similar to Ogden's thesis that "statements about God and his activities *are* statements about human existence,"[37] but it omits his addition of "and *vice versa*.") But these philosophers have also made it clear that "man-statements," or "statements about human existence," are far from being all alike or on a single level. Man is involved in a multitude of language-games, and to take them all as the same game is to produce logical chaos. There is all the world of difference between saying, "The movement of abstract expressionism is dying, I'm told," by one making conversation, and "I am dying," when the medical evidence is clear. To confine ourselves to the language developed by men (and what other choice is available to us?) appears to confine our subject to the realm which is at least in principle open to human investigation, but that does not exclude the richness and variety within this human realm. There are man-statements modeled on nature and the machine, and there are others modeled on the odd word "I." They are hardly the same. If we want to say that, although we are not sure what we mean when we speak of God, our concern is with Jesus

[37] Ogden, *op. cit.,* p. 137.

of Nazareth and with our life in the world today, this concern could certainly be expressed in more than one way. The road ahead is not predetermined, nor is it dull and flat.

Our brief survey of several attempts to interpret the language of faith by means of linguistic analysis does not of itself give us a method for our reconstructive task. It does suggest, however, a basis for understanding the language of faith which can be applied to the biblical and the patristic assertions concerning Jesus of Nazareth, but only a short section in one of Ramsey's books gives even a hint of what such an interpretation of the Gospel might be. The faith-statements which have occupied these philosophers belong essentially to the area of "natural theology" as it was taught in the eighteenth century. The names of Barth and Bultmann are not unknown to them, but the revolution in philosophy of the past fifty years does not seem to have taken cognizance of the revolution in theology of almost exactly the same period. It may be too strong to say that they have been working with the religious language learned in Sunday school, but the theologian cannot help feeling that the most serious problems of faith have not been dealt with when the logical difficulty of saying, "There is a God," or "God exists," is pointed out. Theologians have been saying this themselves for some time. The discussions in modern theology have centered around the kerygma and "biblical theology," while these philosophers have concentrated on the doctrines falling under the traditional rubric of "natural theology." The application of the methods of modern philosophy to the problems of modern theology has been barely begun, and we wish to proceed in this new direction.

For the particular language-game which we are playing, imprecisely identified as "seeking the secular meaning of the Gospel," the heart of the method of linguistic analysis lies in the use of the verification principle—that the meaning of a word is its use in its context. The meaning of a statement is to be found in, and is identical with, the function of that statement. If a statement has a function, so that it may in principle be verified or falsified, the statement is meaningful, and unless or until a theological statement can be submitted in some way to verification, it cannot be said to have a meaning in our language-game.

This means that the context of the language of faith may not be neglected. Any attempt to interpret the statements of theology as though they had been found on separate scraps of paper will be misleading. The words "Jesus is Lord," for example, have no meaning unless they were spoken or written by someone for some reason. We shall have to ask why they were said in a given situation, what they were intended to accomplish. The function will vary to some extent with the context, and as it varies, the precise meaning will change. In one situation, the believer may be reminding himself of his own "blik." In another, he may be trying to indicate to another that he has just this "blik" and not another. These functions are related, but they are not identical.

Linguistic analysis calls our attention to the wide variety of language-games and *kinds* of words. There are situations and appropriate words, for example, which center in discernment, duty, or commitment. Linguistic analysts warn us not to mix the language of such situations with that appropriate to giving "factual" information, for example. To do so is to endanger all understanding, for ourselves as well as for others. There are also words which function in odd ways. "I" is such a word, and the fact that the Christian creed begins with this odd word should warn us to expect the whole series of creedal declarations to be odd. And since this first logical oddity is followed by another, "believe," which points to the language of discernment and commitment, Christians should beware, for example, of a question about "the historic facts of the Virgin Birth and other articles in the Creed."[38] To introduce the word "facts" at this point is to beg for logical confusion and linguistic chaos.

For the sake of clarity, believers should make clear when and

[38] From a protest made to the General Theological Seminary, reported in *The Living Church*, Sept. 17, 1961, p. 6.

how they are using odd words. If "God" is not a word which refers to something, they should be careful not to use it in a way that suggests that it does. If they are talking about a "blik," rather than about "how things are," they should say so. Whatever else may be said about Flew's parable, it must be granted that (following Hare's interpretation) the language of the believing explorer was at least misleading. If he meant something different by the word "gardener" from what his sceptical colleague had in mind, he might at least have made this clear. It would have saved them both a number of sleepless nights.

These remarks on a method of analyzing theological statements reveal that we share certain empirical attitudes with some linguistic analysts. We have not said how far these attitudes take us nor to what degree they are shared, and our use of the word "empirical" has therefore been somewhat loose. It is clear that we have little difficulty with the statement that John is heavier than Jane, and we are reasonably sure of the empirical footing of this assertion. Do we want to say that "John loves Jane" is empirical? We certainly want to say that it is a comprehensible and meaningful statement in a "secular" age, and that this is because it meets certain empirical expectations which we have upon hearing statements about human activities and relationships. But we should also want to say that the empirical commitments of what we have loosely called secularism does not exclude our saying that there is a difference between my saying "John loves Jane" and John saying "I love Jane." The empirical attitudes of secularism, as we are using the term, have room also for this third statement. The further clarification of these attitudes will arise from a consideration of the history of Jesus of Nazareth and the things which the first believers said about him. This is to admit that the word "secular" in the title of this study is itself a function of what we take to be the Gospel.

Part Two

Part Two

V

JESUS OF NAZARETH

The Problem of History

The first proclamation of the Gospel, according to the author of Acts, was a message about "Jesus of Nazareth, a man attested to you by God with mighty works and wonders and signs which God did through him in your midst, as you yourselves know."[1] "The gospel of God," St. Paul wrote, is a Gospel concerning Jesus, a man "descended from David."[2] The Gospel, whatever else it is or has to say, concerns Jesus of Nazareth, and his name has occupied a key position in confessions of faith by Christians from the earliest times. Before pursuing further the relationship between this man and the things believers have said about him, we wish to make the minimal but important observation that the language of Christian faith has always had to do with a particular man who lived and died in Palestine.

This observation is often expressed by saying that Christianity is a "historical religion." Christian faith and the language

[1] Acts 2:22.
[2] Rom. 1:1, 3.

109

in which it is expressed have to do with a man in history named Jesus of Nazareth. An analysis of the language of the Gospel, therefore, will involve us in talking about history, and it will be well if we make clear how we intend to use that word. We shall use the word "history" in the sense defined by R. G. Collingwood. History, according to Collingwood, is an answering of questions about human action in the past. The answers are found by means of the interpretation of evidence, and they are sought for the sake of human self-knowledge. He points out, therefore, that an account of "how God works in history" is not history, for it presupposes part of the answer (i.e. that it was God who was at work, not something or someone to be determined by the interpretation of evidence). It is about God's action, moreover, not man's, and it is investigated for the sake of knowledge of God rather than of man.[3]

Our choice of Collingwood's definition of history for the purpose of our study indicates that we find that it reflects similar empirical attitudes to those out of which this study has arisen. It does not attempt to speak of "God" as an "actor in history," yet it has room for "human self-knowledge." It does not have room for language about transempirical entities such as angels, but it will allow us to speak of the phenomenon of love between men and the difference between a man who is afraid and another man who is unafraid. Other definitions of history may draw other lines around the area within which it is judged proper to speak, but however the lines are drawn, the area within will reveal such a lack of homogeneity as that which lies between changes in the weather, for example, and human action. We have chosen a definition which is open to more distinctions than that, but one which would not appear to be logically puzzling to Flew's sceptical explorer.[4]

---

[3] Collingwood, *The Idea of History,* (New York: Galaxy, Oxford, 1959), pp. 10 ff.
[4] Cf. Collingwood, *op. cit.,* p. 219, for a strikingly Wittgensteinian analysis of self-knowledge as a form of historical thinking.

Let us set beside Collingwood's use of the word "history" some words from Bultmann's Gifford Lectures, *History and Eschatology*. He quotes Erich Frank with approval: "To the Christian the advent of Christ was not an event in that temporal process which we mean by history today. It was an event in the history of salvation, in the realm of eternity, an eschatological moment in which rather this profane history of the world came to its end. And in an analogous way, history comes to an end in the religious experience of any Christian 'who is in Christ.' "[5]

Bultmann closes his book a few pages later with these words: "Man who complains: 'I cannot see meaning in history, and therefore my life, interwoven in history, is meaningless,' is to be admonished: do not look around yourself into universal history, you must look into your personal history. Always in your own present lies the meaning in history, and you cannot see it as a spectator, but only in your responsible decisions. In every moment slumbers the possibility of being the eschatological moment. You must awaken it."[6] For Frank, "history" means "the profane history of this world." Beside this he posits a "history of salvation." Bultmann makes a similar distinction between "universal history" and "personal history." We shall leave aside the problem of the meaning of the word "history" when qualified as "the history of salvation" or as "personal history." For our purposes, however, we are not willing to surrender "history" in the sense of "the profane history of this world." Whatever else we might say about Jesus of Nazareth, he has a place in the realm of human action in the past. We indicate our uneasiness with Frank's and Bultmann's distinctions by saying that we prefer to speak of Jesus having a place in "secular" history. This intentionally indefinite statement again suggests something of the "open texture" of our use of the word "secu-

---

[5] Erich Frank, *The Role of History in Christian Thought*, pp. 74-75, cited by Bultmann in *History and Eschatology* (Edinburgh: Edinburgh University Press, 1957), p. 153.
[6] Bultmann, *op. cit.*, p. 155.

lar," as well as something about our use of the word "history."

Bultmann's words of advice to the discouraged man raise the problem of another expression: "meaning in history." Using "history" in Collingwood's sense, we may suppose that the man who says, "I cannot see meaning in history," is saying that history "says" nothing to him. He can deduce no purpose for his life from the study of human activity in the past. If he were to say that history is only so many "bare facts," of course, he would be revealing that he has some standpoint from which he looks at history. What is the meaning of "bare facts" in the context of human actions, including the act of historical investigation? Even a man who says, "History is bunk," implies that history "says" this to him. But what would he mean if he said the opposite? He might mean that a discernment situation (to use Ramsey's phrase) had occurred when he looked at some piece of history. He might have read the history of the American Revolution, and found himself claimed by it, with the help of Lincoln's Gettysburg Address. "Fourscore and seven years ago our fathers brought forth on this continent a new nation, conceived in liberty. . . ." These words are certainly open to critical investigation by the historian. The historian may wish to say that economic considerations, for one thing, had a far greater role to play than Lincoln's words indicate.[7] Yet such words might lead a man to a certain discernment which would involve a commitment. The result might be a strong sense of national identity and purpose for our discouraged man. He would have found "meaning in history" and, with it, "meaning" for his life. One could suppose another man reading Marx and the history of the Russian Revolution and becoming a Communist. This too would be a clear example of "finding meaning in history," and therewith meaning for his own life.

"Meaning" is not some "ghost in the machine," not some shadowy element which lies in hiding "in" history. "Meaning,"

[7] H. Richard Niebuhr made a similar point in his *The Meaning of Revelation* (New York: Macmillan, 1941), pp. 60 ff.

in Bultmann's phrase "meaning in history," refers to the attitude of the viewer or speaker. It points to *the way in which he sees* history, to the discernment and commitment arising out of his study of one piece of history which influences the way in which he looks at the rest of history and also his own life. Logically, to find "meaning in history" is to have a "blik": an intention to behave in a certain way (in our examples, as a loyal American or as a loyal Communist), connected with the "entertainment" of certain stories (the Gettysburg Address, or the Communist Manifesto). Bultmann seems to have sensed this when he advises the discouraged man to look to himself, that the meaning is in his own personal history. His way of expressing it obscures the logic of the phrase, however, and the result is that he tells the discouraged man that he should stop looking about him altogether. That is like asking a man to have an attitude without reference to the object of the attitude. The word "meaning" does indeed point to a decision (Ramsey calls it a commitment), but it is a decision about something.

Finding meaning in history has two parts logically, which are related in a particular way. There is the history in question, and there is the man who is reading or hearing about this history. The word "find" points to the fact that the man suddenly or slowly begins to see this history in such a way as to feel himself challenged and claimed by it. By using the active voice, "find," and also the passive voice, "challenged and claimed," we indicate the range of ways in which a man might speak of a piece of history which has become significant for him. The former reflects the fact that he is the active member of the two parts; *he* sees the history in a new way. The passive voice indicates that the way he now sees history is new for him. It is an insight which "came" to him, perhaps quite apart from any intention of his other than a mild curiosity about the history he was studying. To say that I am "claimed" by a piece of history is a peculiar use of the passive voice which is related linguistically to saying, "I was gripped by that piece of music," or, "I was seized by the idea." In like manner, a man might say that a piece of history "says" something to him, so that it influences his "blik." His actions and words will reflect his new perspective.

The meaning in history, therefore, cannot (logically) lie "in" history itself, as Bultmann uses these words. But it is misleading to say that it lies "in" man or in his "personal history." The expression "meaning in history" belongs to the language-game of reading or hearing history and discerning it in a way which leads to a new commitment. To speak of meaning in history is to speak of the insight and commitment which has arisen out of or is reinforced by one's reflection upon history. To say that there is no meaning in history is to say that in reading or hearing history, no *new* perspective has arisen which might lead to a commitment. Previously held commitments which might have led a man to say that history is bunk, or that it consists only of bare facts, might have been reinforced. A "bare facts" historian would also be a man with a "blik," though his "blik" would differ from Collingwood's.

The historian's task, according to Collingwood, is to enter sympathetically into his subject, seeking to share in the experiences of his subject. To study the history of Julius Caesar, for example, the historian should try to understand Caesar from the "inside," as it were, as well as from the outside. This act of historical imagination, however, in which the historian tries to "put himself in the shoes" of the figure who is his subject at the moment, does not overcome the difference between the historian and his subject.[8] Collingwood is not talking about something mystical. His language seems rather to be a logical cousin of that which is used in the diplomatic service when it is said that a good foreign service officer can develop "empathy" with the people among whom he is representing his government. He tries to understand them as they understand themselves, according to his human and imaginative capacities; he tries to "see the

---

[8] Collingwood, *op. cit.*, pp. 174, 213.

other person's point of view," without for a moment thinking that he has become in any way that other person.

If we take this conception of the historical task to the problem of understanding Jesus of Nazareth, however, we are faced with difficulties. By Collingwood's definition of the task, we should have to try to enter with sympathy into his history, seeking to understand him from his own point of view, whether as historians or as students of others who had undertaken this work for us. Every attempt to do this, however, including the nineteenth-century movement of "the quest of the historical Jesus," has failed. The difficulty lies not only in the radical difference (which Albert Schweitzer underscored) between the outlook and attitude of Jesus and ourselves, which blocks all penetration into Jesus' own perspective; the difficulty lies also in the fact that the documents available for the study of Jesus' history are peculiarly ill adapted to such an approach. The Synoptic Gospels of Mark, Matthew, and Luke are not records or original documentary sources about Jesus. Modern study of the Gospels has made it clear that the point of view not only of the evangelists, but also of the early preaching of the church on which their work was based, was radically colored by faith in the resurrection of Jesus. The earliest memories and reports of Jesus' life and words seem to have been shaped by the impact of the Easter event and Easter faith. The evangelists were not asking questions; they wrote with the conviction that the proclamation on which their writings were based was an answer, not an inquiry. They did not reach an answer by weighing the evidence. Their subject, moreover, was in part human action in the past, but it was far more the action of "God," and their primary "human subject," Jesus himself, was seen not simply as a man of the past, but far more as a man alive in the present as the ruler of the world. This definition of their subject oversimplifies complex problems, but it registers a second way in which the evangelists were not doing history in Collingwood's sense. Finally, their avowed purpose, however much it had to do with saying something about man, was to make known something about the one they called "God." They wrote as believers, even as worshipers, and if we wish to call them historians, then they were historians with these commitments, which are not identical with those which inform Collingwood's definition on the one hand, or with those of our hypothetical "bare facts" historian on the other. They did not try to "enter sympathetically" into the mind of Jesus, and they have left us little to go on if we take that as the historical task. We shall see that there are a number of historians who feel that the task is not quite hopeless, but the difficulties are clearly serious.

Our interest in this study is not in the historical problems of such a quest of the historical Jesus, however, but in the function of the language of the New Testament kerygma, for even if we form a picture of the historical Jesus, a faith based on this picture would be different from the faith of the apostles. There were no Christians before Easter; this fact may not be forgotten. According to the New Testament, Christian faith first arose in connection with the event of Easter and afterwards in the context of the proclamation of that event. Easter marked the beginning of the faith expressed in the kerygma. If we are to understand the kerygma and the apostolic faith attested by the New Testament writings, we cannot avoid dealing with the problem of Easter. Easter was the turning point in the way the disciples looked at and spoke of Jesus; from that time, they saw him and spoke of him in a new way.

But *that* which was seen and spoken of in a new way was the man Jesus. This fact receives abundant testimony from the New Testament documents. According to the author of *Acts*, the first public proclamation of the Gospel was an address concerning "Jesus of Nazareth, a man . . . [whom] you crucified and killed. . . . But God raised him up."[9] He who was descended from David,[10] the one who humbled himself and accepted death, even death on a cross, was the one who was highly ex-

[9] Acts 2:22–24.
[10] Rom. 1:3.

alted, according to early traditions.[11] According to another primitive tradition, antedating all our written records and said to come from those who instructed Paul, he who died and was buried was also the one who "appeared" to the disciples "on the third day."[12] The one of whom the disciples spoke in a new way beginning on Easter was the man whom they had known by the name of Jesus, a man of Nazareth whose brothers, sisters, and parents were known.[13] Without denying the peculiar relationship of faith to the event of Easter, a subject to which we shall return, let us see what we can say about the history of Jesus as a man. What we include and what we exclude, already suggested by speaking of "the history of Jesus as a man," will indicate yet more clearly the categorical commitments on the basis of which this study is made and the meaning of the word "secular" in its title.

The Historical Jesus

There is no reasonable historical doubt among contemporary Western-trained historians that there was a man named Jesus, a Jew who lived, taught, and died in Palestine during the first third of the first century A.D., and who has been ever since the center of concern of the Christian religion. The nineteenth century witnessed a veritable flood of books which attempted to portray Jesus "as he really was," but the conclusions were hardly consistent. This flood only receded in the first quarter of our century; the turning point was marked by Albert Schweitzer's *The Quest of the Historical Jesus,* which has been aptly called both the monument and the funeral oration of this whole endeavor.[14] The choice left at the end by Schweitzer was

[11] Phil. 2:8–9.
[12] I Cor. 15:4–6.
[13] Matt. 13:55.
[14] G. Bornkamm, *Jesus von Nazareth* (Stuttgart: Kohlhammer, 1956), p. 11. Translation by Irene and Fraser McLuskey with James M. Robinson, *Jesus of Nazareth* (New York: Harper & Brothers, 1960), p. 13.

that either of accepting the evidence that Jesus was so radically oriented toward Jewish apocalyptic thinking as to be beyond our understanding today, or of knowing almost nothing about him at all. Bultmann led the dominant trend of the second quarter of this century in making the second, more sceptical choice. In this he was joined by Barth. Both agreed at least in the conviction that the documents at our disposal do not provide the careful historian with the material for a biography of Jesus, or even for a reasonably probable interpretation of him as a man. A few of the major themes of his preaching, the general location of his activity, and the place and date of his execution at the hands of the Roman authorities are about all that the historian can discover. All the rest—from legends of his birth, through stories concerning his relationship with his disciples, to details of his arrest and execution—has come to us through the preaching of the early Christian congregations. This material was not intended to be documentary evidence of historical or biographical "facts." It was a story in the service of the Easter kerygma.

Neither Barth nor Bultmann has been unhappy about this state of affairs. In fact, one receives the impression that they would be sorry if it were otherwise. Each man's attitude arises from a different motive, of course. Bultmann is unconcerned about the historical and biographical details of Jesus' life and what he may have thought about himself because his interest is essentially in the kerygma of the cross. The historical facts of Jesus' preaching and his death are only the starting point for the proclamation of a new self-understanding offered to men. What Jesus thought about himself is of no help and no hindrance to our hearing the kerygma, and the absence of such historical information is no more to be regretted than our inability to find out how tall he was or the color of his hair.[15] Barth, on the other hand, sees the apostolic witness to Jesus as itself a piece of the

---

[15] Bultmann, *Jesus* (Tübingen: Mohr, 1951), pp. 11 f., 15 f.; translated by L. P. Smith and E. Huntress, *Jesus and the Word* (London: Ivor Nicholson and Watson, 1935), pp. 8 f., 13 f.

history of God's self-revelation in Jesus.[16] What matters for faith is that God has acted, has raised Jesus from the dead (thereby attesting to his own action in the life and death of this man), and has commissioned the apostles as witnesses to this. Nothing more is to be sought behind this once-for-all witness. If one cannot trust these witnesses to God's act in Jesus, what could one trust? Indeed, Barth says, every attempt to go behind the texts has rested on historical presuppositions which have hindered historians from reaching fair conclusions. If the texts are mistrusted because miracles are considered to be impossible, because a priori the resurrection could not have been what the texts say it was, the effort is doomed from the start. For the history that "lies behind the texts" is, according to Barth, just what the texts say it was: the history not of a man, a religious leader, a great teacher, or whatever else the nineteenth century had presumed to see there, but the history of God's gracious act in and for his world. This is the history which matters, and the New Testament has given us all the evidence we need to know concerning this event. Further biographical and psychological information about Jesus would not help us to hear and acknowledge this event, and since the divinely appointed witnesses have in fact seen fit not to give us such information, it is at least irrelevant to that which it is important to know.

Against the background of scepticism concerning the historical validity and theological utility of attempts to construct a history of Jesus of Nazareth, a number of New Testament scholars, themselves students of Bultmann, have begun in recent years what has been called "a *new* quest of the historical Jesus."[17] This movement distinguishes itself from the old quest by the fact that its exponents take into account the critical and theological objections of the intervening scepticism to the work of

[16] For the following, Barth, *KD* I/2, § 14, 3, and § 19, 2.

[17] J. M. Robinson, *A New Quest of the Historical Jesus* (London: SCM Press, 1959), introduces the movement since its formal beginning in 1953 in Germany. A more recent, excellent introduction is that of H. Zahrnt, *Es begann mit Jesus von Nazareth* (Stuttgart: Kreuz-Verlag, 1960).

the past century. None of these men has suggested that the old efforts to write "lives" of Jesus should be renewed. The fact that the basic documents are the products of the believing community and are written from beginning to end in the service of the Easter kerygma is in no way contested. The point is now being made, however, that we may not simply give up the historical problem because of these difficulties. The fact that the kerygma has to do with Jesus of Nazareth, and that the oral tradition which was so important for the early disciples had a great deal to say about the history of Jesus before Easter, challenges us to further historical research. Only, now, as one scholar has put it, we must seek the history in the kerygma itself and the kerygma in that history.[18] The kerygma took in part the form of telling the history of Jesus, and the history itself was told as the good news.

These scholars recognize, of course, that all the reports concerning Jesus were colored and often shaped by Easter faith.[19] They grant that many of them were even produced by that faith. They recognize, however, that faith and the very elaborations of the oral tradition which it produced were responses to the whole person and mission of Jesus. Even sayings that are clearly later additions to the tradition, therefore, are indirect sources for our knowledge of Jesus. The history available to us from the existing documents would not enable us to trace the course of Jesus' career, either externally or internally, but there is a great deal of material which gives us his history in the form of incidents. The task, then, is not to try to write a biography, but to catch glimpses of the man, Jesus of Nazareth. They can be seized from the many little episodes which make up the Gospel tradition. In each of them, the figure at the center stands out boldly, even if we are unable to say just when and where the occurrence took place. From all these fragments, and from the way in which the early church responded to him, the originality and distinctiveness of the figure of Jesus of Nazareth may be seen.

[18] Bornkamm, *op. cit.,* p. 18 (21).
[19] The following argument is essentially that of Bornkamm, *op. cit.*

This new quest of the historical Jesus is too recent for us to be able to speak of a consensus of assured results. It may indeed never come to that, and not all those who are engaged in the quest emphasize the same characteristics. One has focused on the conduct of Jesus, a man who acted neither as prophet nor as teacher, but as a man who dared to act in God's place and as God's son;[20] another has focused on the question of what issue was posed for men by their coming into contact with Jesus, concluding that the issue was that of faith;[21] another has emphasized the immediacy and authority with which Jesus confronted each person and situation, acting in sovereign freedom from the past.[22] These men are relatively optimistic about the possibility of obtaining historical results from the existing documents, assuming that the task of the historian is to answer questions about human action in the past, by means of the interpretation of evidence, and for the sake of human self-understanding. We may continue with this way of speaking of history, therefore, when we consider some of the characteristics of the man Jesus of Nazareth which are noted in these recent investigations.

Jesus of Nazareth was a singular individual. His characteristics seem to have impressed his followers so that he stands out as a remarkably free man in the records of remembered parable, saying, or incident, and in the way in which the early Christian community spoke of him. In describing him with the word "free," however, we would allow that word to take on new connotations from the glimpses of him in the fragments which make up the record. The evangelists themselves indicate this freedom in many ways: they speak, for example, of his "authority," or they point to his openness to friend and foe. Although he is presented as a faithful son of his parents, he is also shown to be free from familial claims.[23] He followed the religious rites and

---

[20] E. Fuchs, "Die Frage nach dem historischen Jesus," *Zeitschrift für Theologie und Kirche*, 1956, pp. 220 f.

[21] G. Ebeling, "Die Frage nach dem historischen Jesus und das Problem der Christologie," *Zeitschrift für Theologie und Kirche, Beiheft* I, 1959, pp. 14 ff.

[22] Bornkamm, *op. cit.*

[23] Luke 2:51; Mark 3:31-35.

obligations of his people,[24] but he also felt free to disregard them.[25] In miracle stories he is even presented mythologically as being free from the limitations of natural forces.[26]

He was called rabbi, teacher, but his teaching broke down the limitations of this title. Unlike the scribes, who supported their teaching by appealing to the authority of the tradition, he did not rest the authority of his teaching on tradition. In spite of the seriousness with which he took the Law, according to some sayings, he was also able to say, "You have heard that it was said to the men of old, . . . but I say to you. . . ."[27] He did not justify his assertions by referring to his own character, his greater wisdom, or his experience. He did not say, "I as the lover of men," or "I in the name of God," but simply, "I say to you." When enemies questioned or friends suggested a basis for his authority, he evaded them.[28] He simply spoke and acted with the authority of a singular freedom.

The content of his teaching reveals this same freedom. He called his hearers to be without anxiety for the future concerning clothes, food, or shelter, and he supported his words with his own conduct.[29] Perhaps the most radical expression of this freedom is found in an incident in which Jesus forgave a sick man his sins, and then demonstrated his right to do this by healing him.[30] One New Testament scholar has commented on this report, that Jesus even dared to act in the place of God![31] He did not leave it to God to forgive men their sins; he did it himself. In this connection we would recall the typical pattern of Jesus' parables, in which statements concerning God and the Kingdom of God are interpreted by stories about wedding feasts, farming, and other human, historical situations, with clear implications for human actions and attitudes. His freedom,

24 E.g., Luke 17:14; 11:42; Matt. 17:24-27.
25 Mark 2:23-27.
26 E.g., Mark 4:35-41.
27 Matt. 5:21-22, 27-28, 33-34, 38-39, 43-44.
28 Mark 11:28-33; 10:17-18; Luke 12:13-14.
29 Matt. 6:25-33; Luke 9:58.
30 Mark 2:5-12.
31 Fuchs, *op. cit.*, pp. 220 f.

finally, is evident in his making no claims for himself. He seems to have been so free of any need for status that he was able to resist all attempts by others to convey status on him.

If we would define Jesus by his freedom, however, we must emphasize its positive character. He was free from anxiety and the need to establish his own identity, but he was above all free for his neighbor. This was the characteristic which Bonhoeffer, in his last writings, found so impressive. He was free to be compassionate for his neighbor, whoever that neighbor might be, without regard to himself. The tradition reveals the impress of this characteristic with its frequent references to his compassion for those who suffered, his openness to all whom he met, his willingness to associate with those whose company was avoided by respectable people. He was reported to have taught that the greatness of freedom lies in service,[32] and his own freedom was characterized by humble service to others. A story like that of his washing his disciples' feet, for which the historical sources are uncertain, illustrates the impression Jesus made on men. The story represents a response to one who could have done this sort of thing, and we can find the basis for such a response in any number of more reliable fragments of the tradition. He was, apparently, a man free to give himself to others, whoever they were. He lived thus, and he was put to death for being this kind of man in the midst of fearful and defensive men.

We have summed up the characteristics of Jesus around the one concept, freedom. Others have used other terms, like "faith." We prefer the word "freedom" to the word "faith" in part because it does not lead us so easily onto the slippery ground of the nonempirical. It could be said that "faith," "faithful," "trusting," are not synonymous with "freedom," "free," "liberated." It might be argued that Jesus was "free" because "he trusted in the God of love." The statement, "He trusted in the God of love," is related in the language of Christian faith to such statements as, "He loved men" and "He was willing to die." It appears to have "cash value" in the realm of human conduct.

[32] Mark 10: 42-44.

Generally speaking, Christians have tended to say that freedom from fear and freedom to love one's neighbor count for the validity of one's making this assertion. He who said he trusted in God, but was afraid of failure or death and was unloving, would be misusing language.[33] Freedom, in this sense, therefore, is not the consequence of faith. It is its logical meaning.

With the particular empirical attitudes which are reflected in the way we have chosen to use the word "history," *we* can only speak historically of Jesus by using words with which we speak of other men. Having spoken of him as an exceptionally liberated individual, we should point out that we might say this of other men. A free man can have an interesting effect on those with whom he comes in contact. He may attract them, or he may repel them, his freedom exposing by contrast the extent to which they are bound by feelings of insecurity, fear, guilt, and by the desire to justify or explain themselves. One could find many examples in history of this reaction to relatively free men. Socrates is an obvious example of a man whose freedom both attracted disciples and threatened others to such a degree that he was condemned to death. Both Jesus' following and his arrest and death can be understood as reactions to what we have called his freedom. As we have defined history, we can go this far in understanding Jesus of Nazareth.

A historical knowledge of Jesus, however, is not faith. We have said that Christian faith and its expression in the kerygma is related to Jesus, but what is that relationship? This question is often posed by asking whether "a historical fact," the historical fact of the life and death of Jesus, can be the basis of faith. The question is not as simple as it seems. What we take it to be asking is this: Is it the case that, for the disciples, and also for the Christians of a later time, faith arose as a result of their looking at a picture of the historical Jesus, either painted on their memories or presented in the proclamation of the church? Is this an adequate explanation of the origin of a man's faith in Jesus? If it were, would not the Christian be at the mercy of the historian,

---

[33] Or he would be a liar. I John 4:20!

so that if historical judgment were to repaint the picture of Jesus, the character or content of faith would have to shift with the historical reconstruction?

This way of putting the question reveals that no simple answer will be sufficient. On the one hand, there were no Christians before Easter. However great personal sacrifices the disciples may have made for the sake of their discipleship, however much they may have loved and trusted Jesus, the fact remains that not one of them remained loyal when he was arrested. The man Jesus, however free he may have been, did not produce in his disciples enough freedom to survive the events of the Passion Narrative. They turned and ran; they lost hope; they were discouraged. The apostolic testimony admits this frankly. When one looks at the sum of Jesus' work with his disciples, considering him either as teacher or example, it must be said that he was a failure. The historical Jesus did not elicit faith, in the sense of the response of the early Christian. His freedom was his alone; at best it was shared only in the most fragmentary and fleeting way by a very few men at certain times. We conclude, therefore, that Christian faith was not, and is not, a direct result of seeing Jesus as a historical figure. We are, of course, not thinking of causality in history and in human relations on the model of physical causality. The word "cause" is used in human relationships in a broader, less restricted way than in an experiment in Newtonian physics. But even with this wider conception of causality, Jesus did not cause his disciples to share in his freedom. In this sense we can say that faith is not based on history.

On the other hand, the preaching which was the prime source of our present Gospels and which is reflected in all the books of the New Testament pointed to Jesus himself, the historical man, as the model of full manhood. The believer was called to test his understanding of, and his response to, every concrete situation in life, by reflecting on the history of Jesus.[34] The demand for obedience, humility, bearing one another's burdens, love, and service is based on an appeal to these char-

[34] E.g., John 16:13-15; Phil. 2:5; I Cor. 7:10; Eph. 5:25; I Pet. 2:21.

acteristics in Jesus himself. If historians could establish, to suppose an extreme case, that Jesus had made an agreement with the authorities to spend his remaining days in the wilderness in silence and let some other person be crucified in his place, thereby revealing that he was as insecure and self-interested as his enemies, Christian faith as the New Testament presents it would cease to be tenable. It would have lost its historical foundation. For this reason, then, we may take the other side and say that Christian faith *is* based on history. If saying this places the believer at the mercy of the historian, then so be it. Christian faith has survived over two centuries of intense and often radical historical study of the Gospels, however, and we would say that it can tolerate the risk of further historical research. Indeed it must, for that risk is the price of centering the Christian confession of faith around a man who actually lived, died, and was buried.

We arrive at a seeming contradiction when we try to investigate the relationship of faith (or the believer himself) to the historical Jesus. This paradox is a consequence of the event of Easter, which stands between Jesus and the believer, as indeed it stands between Jesus and the New Testament witness to him. If our language poses peculiar problems at this point, they arise from the peculiar character of the Easter event. The fact that what happened on Easter was reported always as a radically new event and yet as concerning Jesus of Nazareth indicates the two sides of an apparent paradox: faith is not based simply on a picture of the historical Jesus, but the historical Jesus is indispensable for faith. In order to achieve greater clarity here, we must turn to the event of Easter and the peculiar problems of the language which was used to speak of what happened.

Easter

According to the earliest extant written tradition concerning Easter, in which Paul, some twenty years after the event, recounted what he had received as oral tradition, presumably shortly after his conversion, Jesus appeared to Peter, then to the twelve apostles, then to a number of other disciples, these appearances having taken place several days after Jesus' death.[35] The more developed (and presumably later) tradition, presented in the Easter stories in the Gospels, tells of Jesus' tomb being found empty and then gives details of the various appearances of the risen Jesus to his disciples. At first glance, it might seem appropriate to say that the older tradition simply *announced* the fact of the Easter appearances, whereas the later tradition tried to *describe* them. As a matter of fact, neither tradition speaks of the actual "resurrection." Contrary to the impression left by so-called Christian art, no New Testament tradition says anything about an actual rising. With the word "resurrection," the New Testament points toward the whole event of Easter day: its accounts begin with the appearances or with the already empty tomb.

To say that one tradition tells the fact while the other describes it, however, leads us into difficulties, for according to our ordinary use of the word "fact," every fact can be described. If we speak of Easter as a fact, we shall have to be able to give a description of it. To take the later tradition as a description of the appearances, however, raises far more problems than it solves. Because of the influence of the natural sciences, especially biology, on our thinking today, we can no more silence the questions concerning the changes in cells at death which spring to our mind when we read the Easter story of the Gospels, than we can deny that we live in the twentieth century. (This says something more about our use of the word "secular" and reflects the empirical attitudes which we indicate with that word.) But the moment we start raising these questions, we are led in a direction tangential to the heart of the New Testament proclamation of what happened on Easter. The later tradition, if it is taken as a description, is put in terms which, granting our

[35] I Cor. 15:3-7.

empirical attitudes, lead our attention away from the concern of the apostolic proclamation. The intention of the kerygma is hardly to describe the physical characteristics of resuscitation. A case of resuscitation would in no way require the response of faith. We conclude that the later tradition does not constitute a description of the appearances. How then shall we speak of Easter?

As historians, and indeed as proper users of the English language, we would prefer not to speak of the Easter event as a "fact" at all, not in the ordinary use of the word.[36] We can say something about the situation before Easter, and we can say other things about the consequences of the Easter event, but the resurrection does not lend itself to being spoken of as a "fact," for it cannot be described. We can say that Jesus died and was buried, and that the disciples were then discouraged and disappointed men. That was the situation before Easter. Assuming that Jesus' predictions of his resurrection are a later tradition read back into the record after the fact (an assumption based on a consensus of historical scholarship today), there is nothing in the pre-Easter situation which points toward Easter itself. There is no ground for assuming that the disciples expected anything more to happen. On the other side of Easter, we can say that the disciples were changed men. They apparently found themselves caught up in something like the freedom of Jesus himself, having become men who were free to face even death without fear. Whatever it was that lay in between, and which might account for this change, is not open to our historical investigation. The evidence is insufficient. All we can say is that something happened.

---

[36] I. T. Ramsey, "The Logical Character of Resurrection-belief," *Theology*, Vol. LX, No. 443 (1957), pp. 189 ff., argues for the resurrection as being "an 'object of sense' and more." By "and more," he means that to accept the empty tomb as a "fact" would not be the same as to believe in the resurrection, in the sense of the New Testament. But he wants to have it both ways, for he argues that acceptance of the "fact" is included in Easter faith. We fail to understand the logic of this conclusion, which endangers our whole understanding of the Gospel of Easter by insisting that it is *also* an assertion concerning a body.

The older tradition indicates this "something" with the words "he appeared." Is this to be explained psychologically, or by myth, or in the language of time and space? Let us suppose that the earliest form in which Peter announced this occurrence was: "The Lord appeared to me." In the light of the earliest written forms of the kerygma, we may assume that with words like these, Peter would have meant to say, "Jesus, who was dead, appeared to me as a living person, awesome in aspect, so as to constrain me to call him Lord." This assertion records the image which had appeared "on the mirror of his mind." It tells us that Peter had the impression of seeing Jesus alive and awesome. The use of the passive, "He appeared to me," rather than the active, "I saw him," suggests the "objective" character of the image "on the mirror of his mind": as we have noted, the appearance was unexpected; Peter did not see Jesus as a person for whom he had been looking. "He appeared to me," and "I saw him," however, both record sensations of appearance. We may call them both "sense-content" statements, even if there is a difference in the definition of content.

Statements of sense-content cannot be verified by common-sense or empirical means. That is to say, they cannot be verified by a shared sense-experience, since they do not say what "all of us" can see but only what "I saw." Nor can they be checked against empirical data open to any and every competent investigator who cares to examine them, for again, a sense-content statement is about what "I saw," not about what is "there for everyone to see." Only "I" can record what was "on the mirror of my mind." But this is only to say that sense-content statements are not common-sense or empirical assertions, and more cannot be said against them.[37] The way to verify a statement of sense-content is to see if the words and actions of the person who makes the statement conform to it. The test is one of consistency. If Hamlet claims to have seen his father's ghost *and* to have

[37] For the logic of the following analysis of "sense-content" statements, cf. John Wisdom, *Philosophy and Psychoanalysis* (Oxford: Blackwell, 1957), pp. 240 ff.

learned from the ghost that his father was murdered, his claim
is verified by his setting out to avenge his father's death. His
actions tend to support his claim of what he had seen and heard.
In like manner, Peter's statement of sense-content, which identified the one he saw with a man who had lived a certain kind of
life, is verified by Peter's subsequent life.

We may suppose, on the basis of the evidence, that our hypothetical Petrine statement of sense-content was followed by a
second assertion: "Jesus is risen." If I say, "I saw John in the
station yesterday," a statement of sense-content, I usually imply
an empirical assertion, "John was in the station yesterday." If it
is then demonstrated that John was in fact in another city the
whole day, I might say, "I made a mistake." My mistake, however, was in drawing the conclusion that John was in fact in the
station. My impression of having seen John was still real. It is not
invalidated simply by the fact that John wasn't there. I could
say that my senses deceived me; I would have no grounds for
saying I did not see what I saw.

The statement "Jesus is risen," however, is linguistically an
exceedingly odd assertion. The evidence indicates that the
apostles did not intend to assert a physical resuscitation of the
dead Jesus. The "risen body" was not like the earthly body.[38]
Although it bore the marks of the crucifixion,[39] the disciples had
some difficulty in recognizing the "risen Jesus."[40] If he ate with
them, according to some accounts, he also appeared and disappeared in a most unbodily fashion, according to others.[41] The
linguistic oddity of the statement "Jesus is risen" comes from the
juxtaposition of words from two dissimilar language-games. The
word "Jesus" is a proper name, and we may assume that it
functions as any other proper name would function. Logically,
it would be improper to use the word "is" of anyone who had

[38] I Cor. 15:35 ff.
[39] Luke 24:39; John 20:20, 27.
[40] Matt. 28:17; Luke 24:16, 37, 41; John 20:15; 21:4.
[41] Luke 24:31, 36; John 20:19.

died. But in this case, "is" forms part of a verb which had its logical placing in Jewish eschatology, in the hope and its expression of a future given by "God." The word "risen" was at home in the context of such phrases as "Kingdom of God" and "a new heaven and a new earth," which were used to point to the end and goal of all existence. The assertion "Jesus is risen" takes the name of a historical man and says that he was of the realm of "the end." What sort of verification could apply to such a proposition? Is it even a proposition? Clearly it is not a straightforward empirical one. Bultmann and the existentialist theologians have produced exactly the same logical oddity with the assertion that Jesus is "the eschatological event"; by using an end-word ("eschatological") to qualify a history-word ("event"), they indicate that they are not making an empirical assertion in any usual sense.

Words which point to what we called "the end and goal of all existence" are not words which refer to any *thing*. If a man says, "The Kingdom of God is at hand," we may find the meaning of his assertion in its use. Now the use of "end-words" is to inform the hearer of, or to commend to him, a certain attitude of the speaker. The statement "the Kingdom of God is at hand," taken alone and apart from one who says it, cannot be verified empirically, but the attitude expressed by such a statement is open to verification by considering the conduct of the one who makes the statement. Presumably he would "live for the present," rather than make careful plans for his old age. We have no means of knowing what would count for or against the declaration that Jesus is risen, and granting our empirical attitudes, we would say that it is not an empirical assertion, whatever else it may be. The New Testament writers do tell us something, however, about the thoughts and conduct appropriate to one who would make this assertion.[42] The statement "Jesus is risen," therefore, does not signify a movement from

[42] E.g., Col. 3:1 ff.; Rom. 6:3 ff.; 12:1 ff.

a sense-content statement, "He appeared to me," to an empirical assertion. It is a movement to an "end-word" statement, which is verified by the conduct of the man who uses it.

The Easter Gospel of Peter, in both of its hypothetical statements, tells of an unusual experience. It seems appropriate to say that a situation of discernment occurred for Peter and the other disciples on Easter, in which, against the background of their memory of Jesus, they suddenly saw Jesus in a new and unexpected way. "The light dawned." The history of Jesus, which seemed to have been a failure, took on a new importance as the key to the meaning of history. Out of this discernment arose a commitment to the way of life which Jesus had followed. The validation of Peter's Easter assertion is to be found in the fact that Peter too, according to an old and probably reliable tradition, died on a cross.[43]

Easter faith was a new perspective upon life arising out of a situation of discernment focused on the history of Jesus. The peculiar relationship of this discernment to that history was determined by the peculiar experience which the disciples had on Easter. This was an experience of seeing Jesus in a *new* way and sharing in the freedom which had been his. One might convey better the tone of the disciples' words if one said that on Easter they found that Jesus had a new power which he had not had, or had not exercised, before: the power to awaken freedom also in them. Bonhoeffer's words are suggestive in this connection: "The experience of transcendence is Jesus' being-for-others. His omnipotence, omniscience and omnipresence arise solely out of his freedom from self, out of his freedom to be for the others even unto death."[44] What happened to the disciples on Easter was that they came to share in this freedom to be for the others.

To say that the Easter event was "merely a subjective experience" is to violate the logic of the language of the New

[43] John 21:18-19.
[44] *WE*, p. 259 (179).

Testament witness. Every experience is subjective, by definition. We use the word with a person as its subject. "I" have an experience. A stone does not. This remark is not intended to define an ontological difference between a man and a stone, but to clarify the logic of the word "experience." An experience, however, is always an experience of something, also by definition. The experience of Peter and the others on Easter was certainly their own "subjective" experience. But it was an experience of Jesus and his freedom in a way which was quite new for them. They may still have been attracted by their memory of Jesus. But on Easter they found themselves beginning to share in this freedom, and this had not happened to them before. We might say that, on Easter, the freedom of Jesus began to be *contagious*. The word is used with care. It suffers somewhat from a biological connotation, but we also use it in a figurative way: "He has a contagious smile." In a crowd of people, fear can be "contagious" and produce panic. A child's laugh can be "contagious." It is in this figurative sense that we say that Jesus' freedom from himself and freedom to be for others became contagious on Easter. It carries the sense of our "catching" something from another person, not by our choice, but as something which happens to us. We use it to point to the event of Easter, not of course to describe it.

Reflection upon two further aspects of the Easter Gospel will round out our analysis of the language of Easter: the Easter proclamation asserted that God had raised up Jesus as Lord, and the later tradition emphasized the bodily character of the resurrection. In saying that *God* raised up Jesus, the disciples indicated that what had happened to them was fundamental to their life and thought: Jesus as the liberator had become the point from which they saw the world and lived in it. In saying that Jesus was Lord over the whole world, they indicated that their perspective covered the totality of life, the world, and history, as well as their understanding of themselves and other men. We indicate its scope by calling it a "historical perspective." But it was historical in another sense as well. It was oriented to the history of Jesus of Nazareth. The emphasis of the later tradition on the bodily aspect of the risen Jesus underscored that it was the same Jesus of Nazareth who was now seen in a new way and whose freedom defined the freedom of the apostles. The historical man Jesus was not made superfluous by the Easter event. The relationship between the freedom which Jesus had had and that of the disciples following Easter could be expressed by saying that it was the free man Jesus of Nazareth who on Easter began to set them free.[45] This is reflected in the apostolic assertion that Jesus chose them, rather than that they chose him.[46]

We shall summarize our interpretation of the language of the Easter event. Jesus of Nazareth was a free man in his own life, who attracted followers and created enemies according to the dynamics of personality and in a manner comparable to the effect of other liberated persons in history upon people about them. He died as a result of the threat that such a free man poses for insecure and bound men. His disciples were left no less insecure and frightened. Two days later, Peter, and then other disciples, had an experience of which Jesus was the sense-content. They experienced a discernment situation in which Jesus the free man whom they had known, themselves, and indeed the whole world, were seen in a quite new way. From that moment, the disciples began to possess something of the freedom of Jesus. His freedom began to be "contagious." For the disciples, therefore, the story of Jesus could not be told simply as the story of a free man who had died. Because of the new way in which the disciples saw him and because of what had happened to them, the story had to include the event of Easter. In telling the story of Jesus of Nazareth, therefore, they told it as the story of the free man who had set them free. This was the story which they proclaimed as the Gospel for all men.

---

[45] It could also be expressed by saying, "For freedom Christ has set us free," (Gal. 5:1) or "If the Son makes you free, you will be free indeed" (John 8:36).
[46] John 15:16.

VI

THE MEANING

OF THE GOSPEL

The Gospel as the Expression of a Historical Perspective

The Gospel, the "good news" of the apostles concerning Jesus of Nazareth and what happened on Easter, was proclaimed as news of an event which it was good for men to hear. The result of its proclamation was that many responded with joy and became "Christians." They shared the way of life of the apostles and the apostles' conviction that the history of Jesus and the event of Easter had universal significance. We shall introduce our analysis of the language of this Gospel by comparing the positions of those who first preached it on the basis of the Easter experience, and of those who became believers later. After a discussion of particularity and universality in the language of the kerygma, we shall analyze the content of the kerygma itself in its basic form, comparing our result with other analyses of the language of faith. Our result will then be compared with some typical, central christological assertions of the Gospel and with the "call and response" Christology developed in Chapter 2.

Although our analysis cannot cover every detail of the language of the Gospel, we intend to give careful attention to the central assertions of the kerygma, so that the logic of its language will be clear.

In the last chapter, we analyzed the language of those who experienced the appearances of Easter described in I Cor. 15:3 ff.[1] Faith in the Gospel of the resurrection was not confined, however, to those who had been "eye witnesses" of the Easter event. The apostles proclaimed the Gospel to others, and some of their hearers responded positively. Those who became Christians in this way understood themselves as sharing with the apostles in a freedom defined by the freedom of Jesus of Nazareth and in a new perspective upon life and the world. This experience has been traditionally called conversion.

A man who has been converted to Christian faith does not ordinarily go about saying, "I have seen the Lord." He may say, "I have seen the light," however, and this suggests how his experience at once resembles and differs from that of the apostles on Easter. Theology has traditionally accounted for his conversion not by referring to an appearance of Jesus, as in the case of the apostles, but by referring to the work of the Holy Spirit. It should not be necessary at this stage of our argument to explain why saying that a man was brought to faith and freedom "by the operation of the Holy Spirit" is not an empirical assertion, in any unsophisticated sense of the word "empirical." If a man says this, he may indeed intend to call our attention to certain aspects of how things are in the world, and if we see things as he does, we may also attend to these aspects, which would provide some empirical grounding for his statement. The divine reference ("Holy Spirit") does indicate, for instance, that the new freedom and perspective are received as gifts by the believer and that they are of fundamental importance to him. The divine reference is also at least an indirect reference

[1] Cf. also I Cor. 9:1.

to Jesus.[2] Christian theology, especially in the classical Protestant tradition, has underscored this reference to Jesus by saying that such an "operation of the Holy Spirit" does not take place apart from the "proclamation of the Word."[3] The story of the man who was free for others even to the point of death, and whose freedom has been contagious, is held up to the listener, who is invited to share in this event.[4] In the context of hearing the Gospel proclaimed, the listener may have an experience of discernment. He may "see" Jesus in a new way and acquire a new perspective upon himself and the whole of life. A long tradition of Christian devotional literature has emphasized the act of historical imagination in which the reader is invited to be "present" at the events of which the Gospel speaks, and this imaginative act has also played its part in much of Christian worship. Although the language of conversion differs from the language of those involved in the Easter event, they function in a remarkably similar manner. The difference between the two lies in the fact that the believers' expression of faith depends logically and historically upon that of the apostles.

The language of faith, whether that of the first apostles or of a modern believer, contains an exclusive element: it claims the universal significance of a particular, historical individual, Jesus of Nazareth. In our interpretation of the history of Jesus and of Easter, we emphasized the freedom of Jesus. It is evident, however, that there have been other free men in history. We have already suggested some of the dynamics of interpersonal relations which may result from an encounter with a free man. If our reaction is positive, we may feel attracted to him and we may be encouraged to be more free ourselves, or at least challenged to be more free. Our fears may be calmed simply by the presence of one who is unafraid and free from the fears and anxieties which bind us. On the other hand, our reaction may

---

[2] John 15:26; 16:14.
[3] Typically, Calvin, *Institutes*, I, ix, 1-3.
[4] Gal. 3:1; Heb. 2:8-9.

be negative: we may be threatened by a free person; we may feel judged in our insecurity and bondage. This is an odd experience and if we speak of it at all, we will do so with odd words. We might say that there is a certain mystery about it, a mystery of the depths of human personality and relationships.

Jesus of Nazareth may be distinguished, however, from other men who might have a liberating effect upon men. We must grant a "family resemblance" between the language with which we speak of Jesus and the language used to speak of other free men, of course, in order to be able to describe him at all. Nevertheless, we may use a number of the same words in describing two men without denying that the men are actually quite different. When we compare Socrates as portrayed in Plato's *Dialogues*, for example, and Jesus as portrayed in the Gospels, we may say that both men were "free," but we can also see subtle differences. Two different words for "love," *philia* (the attraction of like to like) and *agape* (a love which makes no distinctions and seeks no return on its investment), may serve to indicate something of the difference which we detect between the two descriptions.

The Gospel, however, is not merely about a free man; it is the good news of a free man who has set other men free, first proclaimed by those to whom this had happened. And it has happened again and again during nineteen centuries that, in the context of hearing this apostolic proclamation, men have been liberated. Their response, which the New Testament calls "faith," consists in acknowledging that this has happened by accepting the liberator, Jesus of Nazareth, as the man who defines for them what it means to be a man and as the point of orientation for their lives. They are "in Christ," which is to say that their understanding of themselves and their lives and all things is determined by their understanding of Jesus. They are a "new creation" in that this orientation to the whole world is new for them.

There is no empirical ground, however, for the Christian's

saying that something of this sort could not happen to a disciple of Socrates. Reading the history of Socrates might conceivably have a liberating effect on a person, who might say that he shared in the freedom of the philosopher. If this were to happen, the Socratic's freedom, presumably, would be defined by the peculiar character of Socrates' freedom. He would acknowledge Socrates as his norm. He would be "in Socrates," let us say, not "in Christ." Perhaps the Socratic, like the Christian, would claim that his was the only valid norm. The exclusiveness of such a claim, as we saw in Chapter 3,[5] would express the firmness of his conviction. Understanding the claim of exclusiveness in this way, we take this to be its meaning.

The language of the Gospel contains not only exclusive claims; it has a universal aspect also. It claims that in the history of Jesus of Nazareth something universal, eternal, absolute, something it calls "God," was manifested. We discussed the difficulties of such language in Chapter 3, but a further consideration is in order. Whether formulated in terms of eternity in time, the divine in human form, or the transcendent in the historical, the Gospel is expressed traditionally in language which has its roots in that of the New Testament and which reflects the patristic doctrine of incarnation. Its earliest and most basic form is the confession "Jesus is Lord."[6] This confession is held to be valid regardless of circumstances,[7] but a believer might say that if he never saw any love among men, he would find it almost impossible to make this confession. In that case, part of the meaning of the confession would be to call our attention to the experience of human love. If we grant that human love or its absence is a part of how things are in the world, we can say that the confession has, in this sense, an "empirical" grounding. Our impression from the New Testa-

---

[5] P. 76, *supra*.

[6] I Cor. 12:3; Phil. 2:11; O. Cullmann, *Die ersten christlichen Glaubensbekenntnisse* (Zollikon-Zürich: Evang. Verlag, 1943).

[7] Rom. 8:35-39.

ment, however, is that this confession implies that the believer is saying, "Even if I never saw any love in others, I have nevertheless seen it in the man Jesus and I recognize the claim of love on me." In this case, the empirical anchorage of the confession is in the history of Jesus and in the actions of the believer. The logic of this confession is at least implied by the traditional assertion that there are practical consequences for the man who confesses the Lordship of Jesus, that Christian faith involves a way of life.

Those who first said, "Jesus is Lord," expressed a particular perspective upon life and history.[8] This confession, ascribing universality to a particular man, indicated that faith constituted a certain understanding of self, man, history, and the whole world, and that this universal perspective had its norm in the history of Jesus of Nazareth and Easter. This perspective upon life and the world was understood not as a point of view selected by the believer, but as a "blik" by which the believer was "grasped" and "held." The perspective of faith was spoken of as a response "drawn from" the believer. The language of the Gospel implies consistently that faith is "given," that the believer cannot and does not want to take any credit for it. By its very nature, faith excludes all boasting.[9]

The issue between those whose perspective on life and history is defined by the history of Jesus and those whose perspective is defined by another reference is notoriously one that cannot be settled by argument. This shows that the function of the Gospel is to indicate not only the norm of the Christian's perspective but also the character of the perspective itself. This perspective cannot be held as one point of view among many. It is not a logical conclusion to a chain of reasoning. Of either of these, a man might say, "This is the position which I chose." The language of faith says, "I did not choose; I was chosen. I did not take this piece of history as the clue to my life and understand-

8 Acts 2:36-42; cf. Phil. 2:1-11.
9 Rom. 3:27; I Cor. 1:27-29; Gal. 6:14.

ing of all history; it took me." The language of faith, by referring to a transcendent element, indicates that something has happened to the believer, rather than that he has done something.

On the other hand, if in response to the proclamation of the free man who has set men free the hearer finds himself to some extent set free, if Jesus of Nazareth has in fact become the historical point of orientation for his own perspective upon history, then this response is certainly his own act also. It is a historical perspective which *he* holds. This paradox finds classic expression in the words of Paul: "I worked harder than any of them, though it was not I, but the grace of God which is with me."[10] This paradox is related linguistically to the peculiarities we have noted in speaking of the effect of a liberated man upon men who are not free. It points to the fact that the new discernment and its accompanying commitment to a way of life is experienced as a response. This perspective arises in connection with hearing the Gospel concerning Jesus of Nazareth and it looks back to him continually as its historical point of orientation. To affirm the Gospel is to express this historical perspective.

The man who says, "Jesus is Lord," is saying that the history of Jesus and of what happened on Easter has exercised a liberating effect upon him, and that he has been so grasped by it that it has become the historical norm of his perspective upon life. His confession is a notification of this perspective and a recommendation to his listener to see Jesus, the world, and himself in this same way and to act accordingly. It is an important perspective and it can be distinguished from other points of view. We may illustrate the difference by comparing the perspective of Christian faith and the point of view of the man whose perspective upon life is founded on the life of his nation. The nationalist understands himself first of all as a patriot and he defines his freedom in the context of loyalty to his country. He

[10] I Cor. 15:10.

can understand the Gospel only as making a relative claim at most. He may allow that there is some freedom to be found in Jesus and in loyalty to him, but it is secondary to his freedom as a citizen. For the Christian, however, the situation will be reversed. His assertion, "Jesus is Lord," expresses the fact that Jesus has become his point of orientation, with the consequence that he is freed from acknowledging final loyalty to his nation, family, church, or any other person and is liberated for service to these other centers of relative loyalty. Because he sees not only his own history but the history of all men in the light of the one history of Jesus of Nazareth and Easter, he will not rest content when his nation, family, or church seek to live only for themselves; he will try to set them in the service of others.

He who says, "Jesus is Lord," says that Jesus' freedom has been contagious and has become the criterion for his life, public and private. As Jesus was led, because of his freedom, into the midst of social and political conflict, so it is with one who shares his freedom. The Gospel asserts that Jesus is Lord of the whole world.[11] This means that the freedom for which the Christian has been set free allows him to see the whole world in its light. When the Christian says that Jesus' Lordship is not limited to the church, he is saying that he understands all free men, regardless of where they may say they have found their freedom, as having "caught" their freedom from the same source as he. He will regard them as the ten cleansed lepers of Luke 17:11 ff., who were all set free from their burden, although only one acknowledged Jesus as his liberator. If someone were to object that Jesus is the Lord and Saviour only of believers, he would be saying that he does not see the freedom of unbelievers with the perspective arising from his discernment and commitment as a Christian. The difference is more than a case of theological hair-splitting. It is empirically significant and it has led to serious human consequences in history.

[11] Matt. 28:18; Eph. 1:20-22; Phil. 2:9-11.

This interpretation of Christian faith is related to Hare's concept of "blik." The language of faith expressed in the Gospel may be understood if it is seen to express, define, or commend a basic presupposition by which a man lives and acts in the world of men. That is why we call it a historical perspective. As Hare has pointed out, a "blik" is not an explanation of the world or of anything else, but without a "blik" there can be no explanations.[12] He appeals to Hume in support of his conclusion that "the difference between *bliks* about the world cannot be settled by observation of what happens in the world." Although the assertions of the Gospel are meaningless if they are taken empirically, they do have a use. As Hare suggests, "The earth is weak and all the inhabitants thereof: I bear up the pillars of it," has a meaning, if it is taken as the formulation of a "blik." As an explanation it would "obviously be ludicrous. We no longer believe in God as an Atlas—*nous n'avons pas besoin de cette hypothèse.*"[13] The "blik" of the Christian finds its adequate expression in the Gospel, however, and it is related always, if sometimes indirectly, to the history of Jesus of Nazareth. This is why we call this perspective *historical*.

Ramsey has suggested how a "blik" arises. It comes out of what he calls a situation of discernment or disclosure, a situation which is seen suddenly in a new way demanding a commitment of the viewer. The languages of revelation, Easter, the "illumination of the Holy Spirit," and conversion reflect just such a situation. The decisive discernment situation for Christianity is Easter and the Easter proclamation concerning Jesus of Nazareth. Men may come to Christian faith in all sorts of ways, of course. A man may have begun to be a Christian from reading the book of Genesis, or he may have come through a more distant point of entry. When he has "arrived," however, when he has heard and accepted the whole of what the Gospel has to say, the norm of his perspective will always be the history of

[12] Hare, *New Essays*, p. 101.
[13] *Ibid.*

Jesus and Easter. Because the sources for this history present Jesus as fulfilling the destiny of his people in his own life, his history receives illumination from that of the people from which he came, but in the last analysis, the Christian will read Genesis, Exodus, and all the rest of biblical history in the light of the history of the Gospels.

Our interpretation has underscored an element in Christian faith not immediately evident when it is considered as a "blik" or the consequence of a disclosure situation. We pointed out that on Easter the disciples came to see Jesus in a *new* way. That implies that they *had* seen Jesus in an *old* way. Their new perspective depended upon prior acquaintance with Jesus as a free man. Even Paul had some prior knowledge concerning Jesus. Conversion to the Christian historical perspective depends in part upon some acquaintance with the history of Jesus. To speak of a sheer discernment, whatever that would be, resting on no prior acquaintance with at least some elements of the situation in which it arose, would be like speaking of a sheer experience concerning which we could not say what was experienced. The various illustrations which we have used along the way make the same point. Lincoln's Gettysburg Address presupposed some awareness of the Civil War and the American Revolution. Hamlet's recognition of his father's ghost rested on prior acquaintance with his father. So Easter faith depended on the disciples' memory of Jesus, and Christian faith requires minimal acquaintance with the Gospel narratives.

Miles has spoken of faith as the way of silence qualified by parables. Certainly the Christian possesses no special sources for the scientific description of the universe. Before such questions as whether there is some absolute being, even "Being itself," which is "behind" or "beyond" all we know and are, some final "ground and end of all created things," he will be wise to remain silent. He may qualify his silence, however, by telling something beside a parable. What he has to tell is the history of Jesus and the strange story of how his freedom became contagious on Easter.

Finally, Braithwaite has taken religious statements to be assertions of an intention to act in a certain way, together with the entertainment of certain stories. As far as it goes, this analysis agrees with our interpretation. We would clarify the "intention" with such words as "discernment" and "commitment," and we would define the "certain way" as a response to and a reflection of the way of Jesus of Nazareth. It is a way characterized by a freedom "caught" from him. We would go further than this, however. In order to live in the "freedom for which Christ has set us free," we need indeed to "entertain" again and again that piece of history, for it does not just provide an encouragement to walk in the way of freedom; it is the context in which the light dawns anew and in which that freedom proves again to be contagious for us. Braithwaite's presentation of the relationship between "entertaining" the story and the "intention to behave" is not adequate to the language of the Gospel of Easter, helpful as it has been in indicating of what sort that language is, because he has not done justice to the historical aspect of the Gospel and has completely neglected the peculiar "story" of Easter.

The Language of New Testament Christology

The foregoing interpretation of the history of Jesus, Easter, and of the Gospel provides a logical account of the language of Christian faith without resort to a misleading use of words. The word "God" has been avoided because it equivocates and misleads. It seems to be a proper name, calling up the image of a divine entity, but it refuses to function as any other proper name does. Circumlocutions such as "transcendence," "being," and "absolute" only evade but do not overcome the difficulty. An interpretation of the language of the Gospel which does not necessitate assertions concerning "the nature and activities of a supposed personal creator," in Flew's phrase, involves discarding some of the traditional language of Christianity, no matter how much other ages have revered this language. When Flew assumes that this language is of the essence of Christianity, he passes judgment on cherished traditions, not on every expression of faith. Nevertheless the question that Flew asks applies: Is this interpretation "Christian at all"? The interpretation must therefore be measured against the assertions of the Christology of the New Testament and of the Christology of "call and response" which summarizes the concerns of the theological "right."

To what extent do biblical-christological statements and our interpretation's statements about Jesus and Easter function in the same way? An important New Testament statement about Jesus is that made by the Gospel of John, claiming that he who has seen Jesus has seen the Father,[14] an assertion which summarizes the New Testament witness to Jesus as the full and adequate revelation of God. This saying occurs in the context of a discussion with his disciples on the night in which he was arrested. One of the disciples has asked Jesus to "show" them the Father, as though something were still lacking in what Jesus has "shown" them until that time. Jesus answers, "Have I been with you so long, and yet you do not know me, Philip? He who has seen me has seen the Father; how can you say, 'Show us the Father'? Do you not believe that I am in the Father and the Father in me?"[15]

"Father" is the word which Jesus apparently used frequently in cases where his contemporaries might have used the word "God." It presents all the problems which arise when we try to analyze the word "God." The further explication of this word, however, is not the only, and not even the best, way to understand this passage, for the passage itself suggests a *via negativa* of an odd sort. The author asks us to stop "looking for the 'Father,'" for we shall not find him and the quest is beside the point in any case. Silence is the first and best answer to questions

14 John 14:9.
15 John 14:9-10.

concerning the "Father." There are "many 'gods' and many 'lords' "[16] but for those for whom the freedom of Jesus is contagious, who have been so touched and claimed by him that he has become the criterion of their understanding of themselves, other men, and the world, there is but one "Lord": Jesus of Nazareth. Since there is no "Father" to be found apart from him, and since his "Father" can only be found in him, the New Testament (and this passage specifically) gives its answer to the question about "God" by pointing to the man Jesus. Whatever men were looking for in looking for "God" is to be found by finding Jesus of Nazareth.

The assertion that Jesus is "in" the Father and the Father "in" Jesus suggests just this transposition of the question concerning "God," which lies deep in the Christology of the New Testament. Whatever can be known concerning "God" has been answered by the knowledge of Jesus made available in the event of Easter. Whatever "God" means—as the goal of human existence, as the truth about man and the world, or as the key to the meaning of life—"he" is to be found in Jesus, the "way, the truth, and the life."

We have no idea what would count for or against the assertion that in seeing Jesus one had seen the Father. Unless we knew already the meaning of the word "Father," how could we verify or falsify this claim? The New Testament, and the Gospel of John especially, insist, moreover, that apart from Jesus we can have only false conceptions of "God."[17] But if this passage is understood as a recommendation to turn away from asking about the Father and to ask about Jesus of Nazareth instead, its meaning becomes clear. We *can* say what would tend to verify a man's saying that Jesus is the key to his understanding and

---

[16] I Cor. 8:5-6.

[17] Matt. 11:27 (Luke 10:22); I Cor. 1:21; John 1:18; 8:19; 17-25. Conversely, "with" Jesus, one has no need to seek a conception of God, a point argued by Luther. Cf. B. A. Gerrish, *Grace and Reason* (London: Oxford University Press, 1962), pp. 76 ff.

living of life. One could ask him questions and examine his actions. One could compare his words and actions with the teachings of the New Testament to see what correlation there was. This would be a subtle business, certainly, but it is not in principle beyond the realm of human investigation. In fact it is exactly what the church has been doing, under the name of "pastoral care" or "the cure of souls," throughout its history.

The passage at which we have been looking is followed by a sentence which deserves attention in this context: "The words that I say to you I do not speak on my own authority; but the Father who dwells in me does his works."[18] This has many parallels in the Gospel of John, for in spite of the author's many assertions of the functional equivalence of "Jesus" and "God," there is also a strong emphasis on the submission of Jesus to the "Father." In the later Christology of the church, this became the basis of the problem of the "subordination" of the Son to the Father.

The verification principle precludes taking this assertion of cosmological obedience as a straightforward empirical proposition. Its function is to say something about Jesus which we have already noticed in speaking of his freedom to make no claims for himself. We called attention then to the characteristics of humility, service, and living for other men. Undoubtedly Jesus believed he was obeying some "one," whom he called "Father," but the Gospel of John, as well as the logic of language, forces us to silence before all questions concerning that "one." We can only follow the recommendation of the evangelist to look at Jesus himself; questions about "God" will receive their only useful answer in the form of the history of that man.

A second important aspect of the New Testament witness to Jesus is seen in the assertion that he is not only the revelation of God, but also the act of God: his history is God's decisive act of love for this world. This idea may be summed up typically in

[18] John 14:10

Paul's words: "in Christ God was reconciling the world to himself."[19] This is a more difficult passage to understand than the one from the Gospel of John because it is so largely a "God"-statement. Its verification would depend upon knowing what to do with the word "God," and that is just the problem. The statement may be taken in another way, however. Does it not suggest that the history of Jesus, including the event of Easter, is the history of a reconciliation of a peculiar sort? Jesus was the cause of division as well as reconciliation among men. As we pointed out, a free man can antagonize as well as attract men, and this was certainly the case with Jesus. He who asserts that the history of Jesus was a normative history of reconciliation means that he is committed to the *sort* of reconciliation revealed in that history. Reconciliation, for the Christian, will always have something to do with the freedom for which Christ has set men free, with being free for one's neighbor. To accept and live such a conception of reconciliation will tend to have serious personal, social, and political consequences, for the Pauline passage has a wide range: the world. The Christian understanding of reconciliation has no limit to its application. It will bear upon all areas of human life, personal and public, local and foreign. It will bear upon the way in which the Christian thinks and acts concerning the relations between nations, peoples, and political groups, as well as upon relationships in his own family. Wherever he sees at work in the world any reconciliation at all like that which characterized the history of Jesus of Nazareth, he will support it, and he will rejoice over signs of such reconciliation accomplished, however partially, as much as he rejoices over the reconciliation with his neighbor which has been made possible by his having been set free for that neighbor.

[19] II Cor. 5:19. An alternative translation, asserting first that "God was in Christ" and then saying that he was "reconciling the world to himself," breaks the temporal emphasis in the verb form. If this alternative reading were followed, the first assertion would be parallel to the "in me" of John 14:10, which we have already analyzed. Only the second assertion would speak of what was accomplished in the history of Jesus of Nazareth.

This verse from chapter 5 of II Corinthians is in the past tense. Then and there, in the history of Jesus, in his life, death, and resurrection, the world was being reconciled to "God." According to the words which immediately follow in Paul's letter, this means that "God . . . did not count men's trespasses against them and entrusted [to the apostles] the word of reconciliation." What can this mean? It cannot be a straightforward empirical assertion, for who can say how the world would be different if men had not been pardoned? We can say, however, how we should treat men if we regarded them as pardoned and accepted in some "final" sense which qualifies all human judging and forgiving. Would it not make a difference in our attitude toward a man who had been found guilty of a crime if we were convinced that his guilt was "born by another," that he was pardoned in some "final" sense? This is another way of expressing the Christian's historical perspective, which leads him to take sides with reconciliation, mercy, and forgiveness and to oppose enmity, retribution, and revenge. Jesus' parable of the unforgiving servant[20] helps us to see the meaning of this perspective and its ethical consequences. The "word of reconciliation" expresses a perspective which leads the Christian to understand and act in the world under the criterion of the freedom of Jesus for his neighbor.

The New Testament frequently speaks of that which "God accomplished" in the history of Jesus by saying that Jesus died for our sins.[21] This has been influential in a theological tradition which says that Jesus became the representative of sinful men by the will of God and suffered the "wages of sin" in their place. Paul said of Jesus that God had made him to be sin who knew no sin,[22] and that in that one died for all, "all have died."[23] The same theme is developed in the Epistle to the Hebrews

[20] Matt. 18:23-34.
[21] I Cor. 15:3.
[22] II Cor. 5:21.
[23] II Cor. 5:14.

around the image of Jesus as the perfect and eternal high priest who became also a sacrificial offering.[24] This strain of the tradition has been important in Western theology, especially since Augustine; it received a particularly clear expression in the theology of Calvin and, in our time, in that of Karl Barth.[25] How are we to understand this language?

We have seen that Jesus' freedom was freedom for his neighbor, that he was free from self-concern and therefore open to the concerns of others. We might speak of his solidarity with men: he "put himself in their shoes"; he carried their burdens. In addition, by daring to regard men classed as "sinners" as forgiven and by proclaiming their forgiveness, he convinced them that they were released from the burden of guilt and the consequences of their acts.[26] But what can it mean to say, "He *died* for our sins"? The emphasis is on his death, but we need to remember that theology, as well as the New Testament, speaks of the "cross" or the death of Jesus as the consequence of his life. "The cross" and other references to Jesus' death became summary ways of speaking of his whole history, as indeed his end seemed to his disciples, after the fact, to have been foreshadowed in all of his life. Since his life was one of solidarity with men, compassion for them, mercy toward their weakness and wrong, it is not surprising that his death, which was the consequence of his freedom to be related to men in this way, was spoken of as a death "for us." His death (which could so easily have been avoided if he had taken the way of caution, calculation, and self-interest) was regarded as the measure of the freedom for which he set other men free. The man for whom the history of Jesus and of his liberation of his disciples on Easter is a discernment situation of prime importance will say, "He died for me, for my forgiveness and freedom." When the

---

[24] Heb. 5:1 ff.; 8:1 ff.; 9:11 ff.

[25] Calvin, *op. cit.* II, xvi, 5 ff.; van Buren, *op. cit.*, Part II, *passim;* Barth, *KD,* IV/1, § 59, 2, *passim.*

[26] *E.g.*, the story of the woman taken in adultery, usually found in John 8:3-11.

New Testament says that he died not only for "our" sins, "but also for the sins of the whole world,"[27] it reflects the fact that Jesus was free for every man, those who did not acknowledge him as well as those that did, and it articulates a perspective by which all men, not just believers, are seen.

On the basis of these considerations, we can clarify the dilemma posed by Bultmann: "Does he [Jesus] help me because he is God's Son, or is he the Son of God because he helps me?"[28] The question as it stands only invites confusion. We may say that Jesus helps me because of "what" he is ("Son of God"), and we may also say that such titles as "Son of God" were given to him because of the help he provided. When we say both of these, however, we are using the words "Son of God" in two different ways and are also playing tricks with the slippery word "is." The problem is more clearly expressed if we ask: Does the Gospel speak of a "saving" event which has happened already and which is reported to the listener, who is invited to acknowledge and give thanks for it (a so-called "objective" atonement), or does it announce the possibility of a "saving" event which takes place in the act of acknowledging it (a so-called "subjective" atonement)? Does the Gospel announce a reality accomplished, or a possibility to be actualized by the hearer? This way of phrasing the question makes it clear that we are speaking about *words* (the Gospel) spoken presumably by a believer.

Now of what precisely does the believer speak? He speaks in part of a piece of history, which is certainly in the past. It is the history of a free man and the peculiar character of his freedom. But the Gospel goes on to speak of the moment in which this freedom became contagious in the Easter event, and the speaker, by his very speaking and by the way in which he does it, indicates that this contagious freedom has also touched him. All this constitutes an invitation to the listener to share this

[27] I John 2:2.
[28] Bultmann, *Glauben und Verstehen* (Tübingen: Mohr, 1952), Vol. II, p. 252; *Essays Philosophical and Theological,* p. 280.

discernment and commitment. Perhaps (but also perhaps not) the listener will "see" for the first time, or he will see again, or he will see more clearly than he has in the past. The light will dawn; he will be possessed of a new way of seeing himself, the world, and all things, and he will "catch" something of the contagious freedom of Jesus.

Now, when was he liberated? Or rather, when will he say he was liberated? He will surely say that he became free at the time he acquired his new perspective. But he will be even readier to point to his liberator. It belongs to the language of a discernment situation that we speak of that situation as containing already ("objectively"), prior to its becoming the occasion of a discernment, what was only "seen" at a later time. As the lover might say to his beloved, "I must have passed you a thousand times and spoken to you a hundred, and there you were, the most beautiful girl in the world, and I did not see you. And then, that night, all of a sudden I realized. . . ." She did not become the most beautiful girl in the world for him only "that night." He will insist that she always was that, and that he, poor fool, woke up only later to the fact.[29] Such is the language of the "objective" liberation of mankind in the death and resurrection of Jesus. To insist that this is incorrect and that the actual liberation takes place in the moment of believing, which is perfectly true in a psychological sense, is to misunderstand the language appropriate to a situation of discernment which leads one to a commitment embracing all of life.

An analysis of the language of the Christology of "call and response" presented in Chapter 2 confirms our conclusions about the function of biblical-christological statements. The statements that Jesus was "called by God" to be the one man who was free to be for all the others, that he "bore the divine

[29] The case of "love at first sight" is a compressed variation. The "prior acquaintance," which we have already discussed, would in this case be prior acquaintance with other people and prior knowledge of the fact of "falling in love," together with at least the first impression of the beloved as a person distinct from these other people.

election" of Israel to be a light for the Gentiles, that his history "was the enactment of God's eternal plan and purpose," if taken to be cosmological assertions, are meaningless in the terms of the empirical attitudes in which this study is grounded. These statements, however, belong after the words "I believe," and the word "I" is important. The statements, in the form of a confession of faith, reflect or suggest a situation in which the history of Jesus has been or might be seen in a new way. They also express the commitment of the speaker to what he has now "seen." To speak of Jesus' "call" or "election" is to speak of Jesus as one with a history which is different from that of any other man, and of Jesus as one who is "set apart" from all the others and for all the others. As the language of one who, in seeing Jesus as the free man who has set others free, has also been set free himself, the statement is appropriate and logically meaningful. This clarifies also the statements concerning Jesus' "response," for his response was only the other side of the coin. To speak of Jesus' "response" is another way of speaking of his history as a free man. Since according to the New Testament his response of obedience was authenticated as perfect obedience by the event of Easter, we may say that it is the contagious aspect of his freedom which authenticates the language which the believer uses of Jesus. To say that Jesus embodies the plan of God and that he was perfectly faithful to this election is to make the sort of final statement which Ramsey says takes the form "I'm I." In this case, however, the "I" is what "I" have become as a result of the liberation arising from hearing the story of Jesus, his life, his death, and Easter.

Finally, the "eschatological" hope, in this interpretation of the language of the Gospel, is the conviction that the freedom which the believer has seen in Jesus and which has become contagious for him, and the reconciliation which he sees to be associated with this freedom, will prevail on this earth among all men. That is his conviction, not a prediction. To say that this hope is "eschatological" is to say that one would die rather than abandon it. It indicates the unqualified, undebatable aspect of the Christian's historical perspective.

As Hare points out, there is no arguing about "bliks." Another man may find some other piece of history to be his key to the understanding of life and history: that of the Buddha or Mary Baker Eddy. Or his perspective might be informed by some idea or ideology. It might be a dialectic of history and the Communist Manifesto, an eighteenth-century Declaration of Independence, or the economic theory of Adam Smith. He who has his freedom from Jesus will not agree, however, with those who would say that all sources of freedom are the same. The fact remains that the history of Jesus is not the same as the history of the Buddha, the Communist Revolution, or Henry Ford. It is one thing to say that Christians have always taken the history of Jesus to be indispensable and definitive for their faith, but it is quite another to think that this "uniqueness" can somehow be proved. Christians have never been able, however (and when they were at their best have not tried), to *prove* the "superiority" of their historical perspective over other perspectives. Claims of "finality" are simply the language appropriate to articulating a historical perspective. The logic of these claims can be illuminated by setting them alongside the statement "I'm I."

The meaning of the Gospel is its use on the lips of those who proclaim it. The Christian has seen a man of remarkable and particular freedom, and this freedom has become contagious for him, as it was for the apostles on Easter. The history of this man and of Easter has become a situation of discernment, reorienting his perspective upon the world. If he should have occasion to tell that story, therefore, he can only do so to express, define, or commend this historical perspective, for this is the secular meaning of that Gospel.

That assertion is itself, of course, a recommendation to the reader to see the language of faith in the way expressed, on the assumption that there is a possibility of his holding empirical attitudes similar to those in the light of which this interpretation has been made. This commendation may also be made in the form of two principles which sum up what we have done:

(1) *Statements of faith are to be interpreted, by means of the modified verification principle, as statements which express, describe, or commend a particular way of seeing the world, other men, and oneself, and the way of life appropriate to such a perspective.* A restatement of the Gospel should allow the logical structure of its language to become clear. With this first principle we indicate that we share certain of the empirical attitudes reflected in the "revolution" in modern philosophy. This principle more than meets the concern of the theological "left" to accept the modern criticism of ancient ways of thinking.

(2) *The norm of the Christian perspective is the series of events to which the New Testament documents testify, centering in the life, death, and resurrection of Jesus of Nazareth.* We have approached the problem of Christology by way of an investigation of the peculiar way in which Christians talked from the first about the man Jesus of Nazareth. Following our first principle, we explored the logic of the language of the New Testament authors concerning Jesus. Our aim has been to discover the *meaning* of their words and to find appropriate and clear words with which to express that meaning today, asking after a functional equivalence between a contemporary Christology and the language of the New Testament. With our second principle, we acknowledge the concern of the theological right wing that Christology be central, and that the norm of Christology be Jesus of Nazareth as the subject of the apostolic witness. These two principles have guided us in the constructive task of interpreting the Gospel in a way which may be understood by a Christian whose empirical attitudes are such as to lead us to call him a secular man.

VII

THE MEANING

OF CHRISTOLOGY

Theology's Responsibility to Its Own Past

An analysis of the function of the language of biblical Christology discloses the meaning of the Gospel and clarifies the issue between Christian faith and unbelief in terms which the contemporary Christian can understand. The New Testament points to Jesus as a man singularly free for other men, and as a man whose freedom became contagious. Its documents were written by men who had received, together with this freedom, a new perspective upon all of life, a perspective which looked to the history of this one man as its norm. They proclaimed the good news of this contagious freedom and of the character and consequences of this perspective, however, in the form of cosmological assertions about the world and the human situation which are meaningless to secular men. To affirm these assertions is to deny the character and tendency of modern thought, which believers share with the rest of their society. What is more important, to affirm them is to affirm only the form and not the intention of the apostolic message.

When we ask after the meaning of the Gospel in this secular age, we are asking after the function of the apostolic message, not its form. We are asking why these things were said, what was intended, what was their use. The function of the language of the Gospel has been demonstrated. It expresses, defines, and commends the historical perspective described. Faith is thereby shown to be the holding of this perspective under its historical norm, rather than a special religious way of knowing arcane information about the cosmos or the human situation. Loyalty to the intention of the apostolic message, therefore, demands our willingness to transform the assertions of the apostolic preaching; indeed, it has demanded this same willingness in every age. Thus in order to indicate more fully the significance of our secular transformation of the apostolic preaching, it is helpful to re-examine the ways in which that preaching was transformed by classical Christology.

Theology as a church discipline has a responsibility to the history of Christian thought, as well as to the Bible. Responsibility to the Bible has been acknowledged in our interpretation of the Gospel by basing this interpretation upon the meaning of the biblical message. Responsibility to the history of Christian thought may be acknowledged by inquiring whether our interpretation is faithful to the intention of Chalcedonian Christology, remembering that, here again, fidelity to intention demands transformation of language.

Re-examination of the language of Chalcedon clearly cannot simply re-establish a formulation of the Gospel which was examined in Part One and found to be useless as an expression of Christian faith for the contemporary, secular Christian. Re-examination can, however, show that since the Christology of Chalcedon, in its time and in its own way, may be judged faithful to the intention of the New Testament message, our own interpretation, in its own way, may be shown to be faithful not only to the intention of the apostles but also to the intention of the Chalcedonian decision. This can be demonstrated, however, only by using the same approach to the language of Chalcedon which was made to the language of biblical Christology. Here too we must be willing to abandon all attempts to refurbish the formulations of patristic orthodoxy unless we wish to deliver the tradition of Christian theology over to complete meaninglessness. To clarify the function of the language of Chalcedonian Christology, precisely by being disloyal to its assertions, is to show that our interpretation is faithful to the Chalcedonian intent.

Such an approach to the history of Christian thought is clearly to be distinguished from both positive and negative evaluations of Chalcedon in its own terms, which were presented in Chapter 2. Here the approach will be to go behind orthodox Christology's own terms and to ask about the function of those terms, in order to show the meaning of that Christology and its relationship to our own interpretation. With this understanding of the theologian's responsibility to the history of Christian thought, let us analyze the statements of classical, patristic, orthodox Christology.

Analysis of the Language of Christology

The Gospel proclaimed by the apostles expressed an orientation of their lives in which the history of Jesus and the Easter event was normative. This historical perspective found another expression among the Greek theologians of the fourth and fifth centuries in the doctrine of the two "natures" of Christ united in the one hypostasis of the divine Logos. The odd duality and unity asserted in that doctrine expressed the odd duality and unity of the history of Jesus of Nazareth: for the Christians, it was both the history of the man Jesus of Nazareth, a part of human history, and also the determining event for their own perspective. This logic of the language of patristic Christology needs demonstration and amplification.

The traditional doctrine of the Incarnation says that God entered the realm of history in the person of Jesus Christ. This is a statement of faith; it will no longer function as an empirical proposition, if indeed it could ever have been said to have done so. The doctrine is frequently cited as the "reason" for taking a positive attitude toward material things, or history, or people. Because, as he says, the Christian believes in the Incarnation, he is therefore impelled to take this world, men, and history seriously. Precisely. His attitude verifies, and therefore gives the meaning of, his faith. The doctrine of the incarnation of the Logos in the realm of human activity points toward history. It expresses the believer's deep concern with history, the world of men, and the world which man investigates; it indicates that his attitude toward men and their activities is related to his attitude toward a particular piece of history. The Christian's perspective is not determined by an idea or an ideal, not by an ideology or a theory, but by the "fact" that a piece of human history has become a situation of disclosure for him. Because this history is that of a human being, the believer's primary concern is with men; his real interest is not in life itself, considered biologically, but in human life. "The Word became flesh," the sort of flesh which "dwelt among us," as one of us: a man with the name Jesus. The Christian is nothing if not one who is concerned for man, and his "humanism" is defined by the history of that man and his strange but human freedom, which has become contagious.

According to the Fathers, that which was incarnate in Jesus was the divine Logos, the eternal Son of God, of one substance with the Father, God of God, very God of very God. It was not some angel, not some created Logos, however high in the order of creation. It was nothing less than God himself. In rejecting Arianism, the believer asserts that his perspective is neither derivative nor in need of further support. It leaves no place for some other perspective on which it might be based, from which it might be derived, or by which it might be supplemented. This rejection of some other "God" who is "above" or "beyond" that which is "revealed" in Jesus is, logically, a "final" assertion of the kind which Ramsey indicated with the words "I'm I." We cannot go further than that. Any suggestion that a Christian's perspective does not have this final character is rejected with his rejection of Arianism.

The rejection of Arianism took the form of the confession or creed of Nicaea. If this confession is considered as a doctrine about the nature of "God," there is no better way open for us now than to meet all questions with what Miles called the way of silence. The Nicaean Creed, however, was written to resolve a problem in Christology: the relationship between Jesus of Nazareth and God. This fact suggests that its authors were defining the basis of their historical perspective. When the confession is understood in this sense, its trinitarian structure is significant. First, Christian faith consists of a single, complete orientation to the whole world. Second, this orientation is that of a life lived in freedom and love for men, which has its norm in the history of Jesus of Nazareth. Third (and here we include the later development of the third article, concerning the Holy Spirit), the Christian acquires this orientation by being "grasped" by its norm. When this happens to him, he becomes free to acknowledge this norm and to live accordingly.

It may be objected that we have discussed only the language of the doctrine of the "economic Trinity" (the way in which the triune God is related to creation) and said nothing about the "essential Trinity" (the way God is "in himself"). The assertion that God is "essentially" and not just "economically" triune, however, is the declaration of faith that God really is as he has shown himself to be, that his self-revelation is to be trusted. If the doctrine of the essential Trinity has a function, it is to define faith as a "blik," in contradistinction to an "opinion" which might be held in a provisional way. Of course a man may be converted out of one perspective into another, but as long as he has a particular "blik," the world he sees through it is for him the world as it "really" is.

We may now clarify the christological assertion that the

Logos or divine Son is "eternal," that the believer is unable to say that there was "a time when he was not." The word "eternal" will not function empirically, but the Christian perspective is in no sense a cosmological, astronomical, geological, or biological theory. It is a way of seeing the world about us, specifically, the world of men and human activity. For the believer, the world he sees is the world as it "really" is. In this sense, the Christian may be expected to say that the world was "always" this way. According to the lover, the beloved did not suddenly become beautiful; what changed was his perspective. Consequently, he will say that she was always beautiful. It is with language like this that Christians express their conviction that their criterion of human existence (which they have seen concretely in Jesus of Nazareth) was always the norm of human existence. To deny this christological assertion would amount to saying that one had abandoned the Christian historical perspective for another.

The eternal Son, without ceasing to be God, became flesh: the man Jesus of Nazareth. The Christian's orientation is defined by the history of this man and of Easter. If Easter is omitted, leaving only a "historical Jesus" who has not set men free, then it is unlikely that this history will become the occasion for discernment. But if it is told as the history of him whose freedom is powerfully contagious, then the listener may be grasped by it. Then the final thing which he can say to "explain" himself, "I'm I," must be expanded to include this history of Jesus, for it is in his light that the believer sees light, including whatever light he has upon the word "I." This means that the Christian will be liable to use "final" words in speaking of Jesus, words of wonder, awe, and worship. And why not? If the historical perspective which is expressed by Christians even when they say, "I'm I," is in fact determined by his history, if Jesus of Nazareth is the norm even of that statement, then their use of the language of praise and adoration is perfectly appropriate. God of God, Light of Light, very God of very God.

"Worthy is the Lamb who was slain, to receive power and wealth and wisdom and might and honor and glory and blessing!"[1]

Very God of very God. But also, very man, consubstantial with us according to his humanity. This is the other side of the Christology of the Fathers and Councils, which points to Jesus of Nazareth as a man, a historical figure in every sense of the word. Theology, if it is consistent with its own assertions concerning revelation, has no prior basis for knowing what man "ought" to be. It cannot, according to the New Testament, circumvent Jesus and go back to Adam, for even Adam is interpreted and understood (in chapter 5 of Romans, for example) in the light of him who is called the Second Adam.[2] To call Jesus the Second Adam is another way of saying that he defines for faith what it is to be a man, what man was made to be, just as he is also called the "new man," indicating the goal of human life. We would emphasize, along with many contemporary interpretations of Christology, that the Christian perspective sees the "true nature" of man in precisely the freedom for the others which was Jesus' own. *Human* being is being free for one's neighbor.[3]

Jesus, as true man, was like us in all things except sin. The New Testament, as we have seen, bases its assertion of the perfect obedience of Jesus to the one he called "Father" on the Easter event. To what extent this obedience or "sinlessness" was recognized before Easter is a matter of conjecture, for the records were written after Easter, and they look back upon Jesus' history in the light of that event. In asserting that Jesus was like us in all things, classical Christology pointed to the fact that Jesus was a man. When it asserted that he was without sin, it pointed to his freedom. We have said that there have been other free men, and we granted that, simply on the historical

---

[1] Rev. 5:12.

[2] Rom. 5:5-21.

[3] Cf. Luther, *The Freedom of a Christian*; Bonhoeffer, *WE*, p. 259 (179); Barth, *KD*, III/2, § 45, 1; IV/2, § 64, 3.

evidence, Jesus cannot be demonstrated to have been more free than any other man, even if the characteristics of his freedom can be distinguished. That which sets Jesus apart from all other men for the Christian is Easter, as the result of which the Christian finds himself committed to understanding all other men in the light of Jesus, and not vice versa. It is this acknowledgment of a norm which is expressed in speaking of Jesus as sinless. The theological assertions that Jesus was "able not to sin," or even that Jesus was "not able to sin," are both related to the logic of the language of discernment and commitment. The first assertion expresses the freedom of Jesus in contrast to the bondage of other men, especially of the one who makes this assertion, and the second points to the unqualified nature of a perspective for which Jesus is the definition of a free human being. Because the phrasing of the second assertion (*non posse peccare*) seems to threaten the idea of freedom, however, the former (*posse non peccare*) is to be preferred. Its logic is less likely to be misunderstood.

The stories of the virgin birth of Jesus may seem to conflict with the insistence of the New Testament on the likeness of Jesus to all other men. As a matter of fact, the nativity stories play only a minor role in the New Testament: they occur in only two of the Gospels, in two different forms; they seem to have been either unknown or of no interest to all our other sources for reconstructing the beliefs of the early Christian community. If they were taken as historical accounts, they would be open to all the problems of the stories concerning the empty tomb, with the significant additional problem of lacking any wide textual endorsement. For Paul, Mark, John, and others, everything that needed to be said about Jesus could be said without reference to a miraculous birth. Some of these sources do speak of his birth, however, at least in passing,[4] for it is natural to mark the birth of a figure of historical importance.

[4] John 1:9-11, 14; Gal. 4:4.

If the man in question is as significant as Jesus is for the Christian, this commemoration is bound to be rather special. Considered as the language of thanksgiving, awe, and joy over the fact of the coming into being of this man, the nativity stories of Matthew and Luke are appropriate and appealing. If it were insisted that they must be understood "factually," of course, they would have to be rejected, for such an interpretation would indeed threaten the doctrine of the full manhood of Jesus specified in the Christology of Chalcedon. But the believers, sharing the wonder and thanksgiving of the shepherds (or of the astrologers in the other story), will not want these stories to be excised from the whole witness of the New Testament. As the angel said to the shepherds, "This shall be a *sign* unto you." The story of the babe born in total poverty and weakness may be an occasion for the deepening or renewal of the Christian perspective, a sign pointing to the life of freedom in the midst of fearful men which ended on the cross.

According to classical Christology, the human "nature" of Jesus had no independent existence, considered apart from the existence of the incarnate Word; it was anhypostatic. This idea was expressed positively by saying that the human "nature" had and has its existence in that of the Logos, in which it exists enhypostatically. The meaning or function of this assertion is to say something about the relationship, in the Christian perspective, between the free man Jesus and the contagiousness of that freedom. The first form of this doctrine means that the free man Jesus has no compelling interest for the believer apart from the consequences of Easter. If the story had ended with his death, had the apostles not been liberated from their fear on Easter, Christian faith could not have arisen. But orthodox theologians finally decided that the proper use of this doctrine was in its second, positive form. Anhypostasia was an improper, enhypostasia a proper, expression of this doctrine. Its meaning is that the Christian can only conceive of Jesus of Nazareth as a man whose freedom has become contagious. For the believer to

be interested in Jesus apart from the contagiousness of his freedom would be to jump out of his "blik." That would be like
"jumping out of one's own skin" (an expression that indicates
something of what is involved in a historical perspective). The
Christian's interest in the historical Jesus of Nazareth is his
interest in the one who defines his historical perspective, the
one who has become his liberator.

The two "natures" of Christ, the divine and the human,
form a perfect union in the hypostasis of the Logos: they are
united, according to the formula of Chalcedon, inseparably and
indivisibly. The language of the perfect unity of the two "natures" of Christ functions according to the logic of the language
in which the relationship of the perspective of faith to the history of Jesus is expressed. The historical perspective which
marks the Christian, and which is his "blik," arises out of the
peculiar way in which he sees Jesus; or, to put it otherwise, it is
based upon Jesus seen in a certain way. There are two elements
in this complex. One element is Jesus as a figure in history having his own peculiar freedom. The other element is the discernment and the contagious power of this freedom which the
disciples experienced on Easter. These two elements are inseparable in Christian faith. The freedom which has become contagious is that of the historical Jesus, and the freedom of Jesus
is that freedom which became contagious. Or, in other terms,
there is no perspective not bound to a particular piece of history, and this piece of history is of interest solely because it has
led to a new perspective. Just as the title "Christ" had already
in the New Testament period become part of the name of Jesus,
so the two aspects of Christology, the divine and the human,
point together to the one reality of Jesus as the occasion of a
historical perspective. The inseparable unity of the freedom of
the man Jesus with the fact that first the apostles and then other
believers have been set free and have come to participate in his
freedom found expression in the doctrine of the inseparable
unity of the two "natures." The rejection of a Nestorian separa-

tion of the divine and human "natures" was, as our functional analysis shows, important to state the Gospel fully at that time.

According to the rest of the Chalcedonian formula, the divine and human "natures" remain unchanged and unconfused in this perfect union. The divine remains divine and the human remains human. This is a further definition of the Christian historical perspective. The freedom of the believer is not the same as the freedom of Jesus; his perspective is not the same as the history on which it is based. The history of Jesus remains a piece of quite ordinary history, open to ordinary historical investigation. It does not become a sort of super-history by virtue of the perspective to which it has given rise, nor is the freedom of Jesus beyond all historical comprehension because it has proved to be contagious for the Christian. However closely they may be bound together, both logically and historically, a perspective is a perspective and history is history. In other words, the history of Jesus remains a piece of human history, and the event of Easter and succeeding occasions of conversion are discernment situations. When an ordinary situation becomes an occasion of discernment for a man, the change lies in the viewing, in what now becomes clear, in the light breaking; it is not an empirical change in the situation. All the physical facts remain the same, even if they can never seem quite the same to him again. This is not a metaphysical paradox; it is the expression of a change in a way of seeing. The change is logically and historically significant, however: it marks the difference between faith and unbelief.

The Antiochene (and in Protestantism, the Reformed) rejection of the Alexandrian and Monophysite tendency to see the human "nature" absorbed into the divine, and the Western reservations concerning the idea of the deification of man in certain elements of Eastern theology, represent a concern for preserving the historical basis of the Christian perspective and for insuring that it be not lost by absorption into that perspective. To compromise here would open the way to a perspective which was not based on concrete human history. Consequently the perspective might be focused only upon the self or upon religious experience, losing sight of the world about us. The Monophysite tendency in classical Christology, latent in an understanding of Jesus as "more than a man," is reflected in the lack of concern about social and political issues so often evident in the church of the past and present.

The Function of Christology

We have found no simple correspondence between patristic christological terms and those of our own interpretation. There is a logical equivalence, however, of these two interpretations of the New Testament witness to Jesus Christ. Roughly speaking, we have placed the doctrine of the human "nature" of Christ in the context of language appropriate to the history of a free man, and this line of thought is relatively straightforward. On the other hand, we have placed the doctrine of the divine "nature" in the context of language appropriate to a freedom which has been contagious, and to the historical perspective which arises from a discernment situation. Here the logic is more complex. This oversimplifies the picture, for before they were ever written down, the stories of Jesus' freedom already reflected its contagious quality, since those who told his story had been liberated and had acquired the perspective of faith. When a Christian says that Jesus was a man, that is historical language. When he says he "is true man," he is indicating that Jesus is, for him, the measure of all men, and this leads already to the other side. The assertion that Jesus is the Son of God functions somewhat as the assertion "I'm I." The concrete reference to the man Jesus indicates that even the word "I" is defined by the history of that man. The discernment of the Christian includes also understanding himself. His final explanation of himself and his actions, "I'm I," may also take the form, therefore: "I am what I am because of Jesus Christ," or "by the grace of God I am what I am."[5]

The confession that Jesus is the Son of God says also that the freedom which the apostles gained on Easter derives from Jesus' freedom. This assertion expresses the perspective which shapes a Christian's thinking and which determines his particular way of seeing the world and acting. The assertion of the divinity or Lordship of Jesus means that the believer no longer puts himself at the center of his picture of the universe, but is now at least to some extent free for his neighbor. The function of the language of Christology is to define this historical perspective and to indicate its roots in the history of Jesus of Nazareth and in the proclamation of the Gospel of Easter.

We may conclude by discussing how our interpretation meets the concerns of the various tendencies in contemporary christological discussion. The theological "right," as we saw, demands that Christology, not soteriology, be primary, that theology make clear the "objective fact" of God's act in Jesus Christ, without losing sight of it in the appropriation of the benefits of Christ by the believer. That which is decisive for man has happened already long before man becomes aware of it and assents to it in faith. We were "saved" some nineteen centuries ago. To this we say, "Amen." The Christian Gospel is the news of a free man who did not merely challenge men to become free; he set men free. The disciples were not merely challenged to make the cross their own, to understand themselves as men who were dead to their past and alive to their future. They were not called to make a decision upon which their whole destiny would rest. No, something happened to them before all that. To their surprise and consternation, and then to their joy, they received a new perspective upon Jesus and then upon all things. At the

---

[5] I Cor. 15:10. The word "grace" may be used in a typical Pauline sense to refer to God's act of love toward men in the life, death, and resurrection of Jesus (Cf. II Cor. 8:9). Here it has also the meaning of God's particular mercy to Paul in opening his eyes to see Jesus in a new way (I Cor. 15:8-10).

same time, they found that something else had happened to them: they became free with a measure of the freedom which had been Jesus' during his life. They expressed this by saying that Jesus had received a new power on Easter to set men free. It seemed to them that they had stumbled on a great truth, which was true before they came to see it. It was, in this sense, "objective." The decisive event was one which they felt had happened to them, and which alone made it possible for them to "decide." Both the language of history, which refers to the past, and the language of a historical perspective freshly gained, support the "objective" emphasis of conservative theology.

The theological "left" has urged us to think through Christian faith in the light of the critique of modern thought. Again, "Amen"; but we would take this demand seriously. It will not do simply to translate the difficult word "God" into some highly or subtly qualified phrase such as "our ultimate concern," or worse, "transcendent reality," or even, "the ground and end of all things." These expressions are masquerading as empirical name tags, and they are used as though they referred to something, but they lead us right back into the problem of ancient thought, or they put us in the worse situation of speaking a meaningless language. Light can be thrown on the assertions of ancient thought, however, and help can be found in finding a way to speak which is honest and loyal to the way we think today, by a careful analysis of the function of the words and statements of Christian faith. We may learn what sort they are, and their meaning, which is their use, will become clear. In this way, we more than meet the concerns of Bultmann and Ogden, even if we do so in a way quite different from that which they suggest, and with rather different results.

We objected to the position of the existentialist-theological "left" on five counts, and it may clarify our interpretation of the language of the Gospel if we compare it with that of the left wing on these same points. We have not had to attempt to speak of God analogically or indeed in any other way, for where existentialist theologians would speak of "experienced nonobjective reality," we have spoken of situations of discernment, including a necessary prior acquaintance with important features of these situations, and we have spoken of a contagious freedom. By taking our models exclusively from the area of human experiences which do not require transempirical language, we are not faced with the difficulty of using circumlocutions for the word "God" which, given our secular empirical attitudes, we find exceedingly difficult to place. Admittedly, words such as "free," "love," and "discernment" are not empirically grounded in the same way as are "undiluted," "gravitational attraction," and "sense data." In developing a *secular* meaning of the Gospel, however, we are suggesting that secularism be conceived as able to contain a language employing the first person singular pronoun.

We have interpreted the language of the Gospel having to do with "how things are" as just that: language expressing how things are for, and what has happened to, a man who sees a certain piece of history in a certain way. This is certainly close to the existentialist-theological interpretation of the Gospel, but an important difference is evident in the fact that the history of Jesus of Nazareth is central in and integral to our interpretation, and in the further point that the key to the relationship between faith and Jesus is placed where the New Testament places it: in Easter. As we said at the very beginning, Bonhoeffer hoped that a "non-religious interpretation of biblical concepts" would both overcome the weakness of liberal theology and at the same time do justice to its legitimate question. Our method is one which never occurred to Bonhoeffer, but our interpretation may nonetheless serve to justify his hope.

VIII

THE MEANING

OF THEOLOGY

Revelation, Predestination, and Creation

A responsible reconstruction of Christology should indicate
its implications in sufficient detail to make clear the possibilities
and limitations of its method. We shall therefore draw the consequences for the principal doctrines of theology which follow
from our interpretation of the Gospel and Christology by means
of linguistic analysis. It is not necessary to explore all the possibilities which more detailed analysis might bring to light, but
we should consider briefly the most important Christian doctrines. Traditionally, the answer to the question concerning
God is said to be given by the whole of theology. In like manner, our interpretation of the Gospel as the expression of a
historical perspective will be clarified by an analysis of the major
doctrines of Christian faith.

REVELATION The God of Christian theology has always been understood as a God who has revealed himself. The
fact that this revelation is situated in the history of Jesus, with

its context in the history of Israel, indicates just which history is decisive for the Christian perspective. Whether God really is as he is revealed in this history, is a question which asks whether the Christian perspective is indeed one of those presuppositions which are the basis of all explanations of the world (although it is not itself an explanation, as Hume recognized). To qualify the answer would be like saying that faith is a point of view which sheds light on the problems of human life, but that life is to be understood actually on some other basis. The doctrine of revelation therefore reflects the very heart of Christian faith.

The traditional doctrine of revelation maintains a particular relationship between revelation and reason. Conservative Protestant theology, like Catholic theology, has never accepted the irrationality of faith and revelation; it insists that what is known by means of revelation is never contrary to "right reason." Reason enlightened by faith is reason functioning properly. The "truths of revelation" cannot be discovered by reason alone, but once they are discovered, they are susceptible to rational analysis and they are logical in structure.[1]

This doctrine corresponds to the rational element in the Christian historical perspective. It is not logically or psychologically necessary that the record of Jesus' history and Easter become an occasion of discernment: it has happened for some men and not for others; it has happened for one man at certain times and not at others; it cannot be "proven." Yet once the believer has "seen the light," he is called to use all his logic or thinking (including his imagination) to see the bearing on his own situation of the history referred to in the Gospel. A high degree of conscious reflection may be needed for a man to see how the reconciliation attested in the Gospel history bears upon the relations between people or nations.

"Faith" always involves thinking. A call to faith that depreciates thinking and logical reflection is a call to a quite different

[1] Thomas Aquinas, *Expos. de Trin.*, qu. 2, a. 2; *Summa Theol.*, I, qu. 12, a. 5, 13; qu. 32, a. 1; II, 2, qu. 2, a. 3; Calvin, *Institutes*, III, ii, 2; Barth, *KD*, I/1, § 6, 4.

sort of "blik" from the one of which we have been speaking. It would be a perspective without historical foundations, a feeling or orientation which could give no logical account of itself. As such, it would be inadequate both to its subject matter and to the demands of contemporary thought, for Christian faith is inseparably related to history, and history requires reasoning.

P R E D E S T I N A T I O N The doctrine of predestination or election has had a renaissance in modern theology. Barth has renewed this doctrine by saying that God's election of Jesus of Nazareth as his faithful son includes also the election of all other men.[2] This teaching is a development of Ephesians 1:3 ff., in which election is given a christological basis; Jesus is both the man elected for all other men, and the man rejected for the sins of all men. The double aspect of the traditional doctrine of predestination is preserved, but because the doctrine is centered in Jesus himself, the old idea of orthodoxy, in which some men are presumed to have been elected for salvation and others predestined to damnation, is overcome. The older form of this doctrine said that God chose some men only, whereas the newer form says that God, in choosing one man only for the sake of all men, has chosen all men.

The difference between saying that God chose some and saying that he chose all lies in a different attitude toward men, and in what is thought to be the most significant thing about them. The old doctrine of double predestination tends to make a distinction between men on the basis of their response to the Gospel. Calvin, who formulated this doctrine classically for conservative Protestantism (a doctrine which he inherited from the Catholic tradition), admitted that he was trying to find an adequate way to distinguish believers from those who reject the Gospel.[3]

Although theology has hesitated to identify believers with

---

[2] Barth, *KD*, II/2, § 32, 33.
[3] *Institutes*, III, ii, 30.

the elect, it has tended to do so, reflecting a belief that God loves those who respond to him. Love is for those who respond to it, and so the most significant thing about a man is whether he is a Christian. It is not necessary to draw the line sharply; a man who thinks this way may allow that he is not the final judge of who is a Christian. He may say that some who appear to be Christians are not elect, and some who appear to be unbelievers are, but his general attitude indicates that, for him, believing or not believing is the decisive thing about men, and his conduct toward unbelievers likely will differ from that toward believers. His perspective suggests that it is grounded finally on his own religious experience, on the fact that he has become a believer, however much he may appeal to biblical texts to justify his position.

Barth's interpretation of this doctrine, on the other hand, tends toward universalism (even if he refuses to admit an explicit universalistic conclusion). He says that God loves not only those who love him, but also his enemies, those who reject his love. In the light of the cross and Easter, love is for man as man, regardless of his response. God loves all men, and Christian love is also for every man, including one's enemies. The most important thing about a man is therefore simply his manhood. It is an indication of the logic of the problem that Barth's interpretation has been well received among Christians concerned with politics and other secular matters, and has been vehemently rejected by members of pietist churches. It represents a perspective grounded in the history with which we have been concerned and not in the religious experience of the believer. The two positions are each internally consistent, but their historical bases differ, and this leads to differences in attitude, intention, and action. The Christian historical perspective is more adequately expressed by universalism than by its denial.

CREATION "I believe in God the Father almighty, maker of heaven and earth." The doctrine of Creation concerns God and his activity, but theologians abandoned long ago the claim that it explains the physical origin of the world. The doctrine is used now to assert that this world—all we have to deal with as men, including life and matter, men and things, and all the forces and powers of the realm of time and space—is God's, that it is his handiwork, and, therefore, that it is "good." The doctrine expresses in fact an affirmative view of the world of men and things.

Recent studies of the creation stories in Genesis show that they were shaped by Israel's experience of the Exodus, and in their present form they express the Israelites' understanding of themselves as the people of the Covenant.[4] Because the Israelites saw themselves as a people brought into national existence "out of nothing" by the event of the Exodus, they came in time to see everything in the light of this event. Yahweh was not only their creator; he was the creator of everything else. Faith in God as Creator of the world was a corollary of their historical perspective. In like manner, the Christian doctrine of divine creation of all things "through Jesus Christ" is a corollary of the Christian perspective. It is only another way of expressing the Christian's affirmative attitude toward the world (as opposed to a dualistic or world-denying attitude) and his refusal to allow anything in the world, except the biblical history centering in the history of Jesus of Nazareth, to determine his orientation. If anything else did, his orientation would be "idolatry."

PROVIDENCE The doctrine of Providence is a corollary of the doctrine of Creation: God has not only made this world, but he directs its course toward an appointed goal. In ancient times, the misfortunes of the wicked and the prosperity of the pious were cited to support this doctrine, but it was soon realized that the evidence of history is ambiguous and calls for many qualifications. If the doctrine of Providence is interpreted

[4] G. von Rad, *Das erste Buch Mose,* pp. 7-13, 15 f., 34.

as a philosophy of history, saying that a nation or individual is
punished by the consequences of its or his stupidity and evil, it
can hardly be made to fit every case and still have any empirical
meaning. As Braithwaite says, an assertion which is compatible
with every conceivable set of circumstances is not an empirical
assertion. Taken as the expression of a view of the world, however, the doctrine of Providence is significant as an assertion of
the strength of the grasp that the Christian's perspective has on
him. This is the meaning of the Christian's assertion that nothing can separate him from the love of God in Christ.[5]

Sin, Justification, and Sanctification

SIN According to Christian doctrine, man was created good,
but he has turned away from the source of his life; he has fallen
into the way of disobedience. Born with a tendency toward
"sin," he allows himself to be the key to his perspective, seeking
his own welfare at the expense of his neighbor. The traditional
biblical text for this doctrine is the story of the "Fall" in chapter
3 of Genesis; the doctrine of the Fall and of man's "original sin"
is explicit in surprisingly few passages of the New Testament,
considering its significant role in the history of Christian
thought.[6] It is implicit, however, in many of the apostolic writings, especially in the recurring picture of man as a creature in
bondage to forces or powers beyond his control.[7] The conception of sin as moral perversity and ethical wrong, which has
marked Western theology since Tertullian, ignores the portrayal
in many parts of the New Testament of man as a creature suffering in bondage. Although the Gospel calls for repentance, it
also proclaims liberation.

Christian doctrine has not been alone in saying that there is

---

[5] Rom. 8:39.
[6] E.g., I Cor. 15:21-22; Rom. 5:12-19.
[7] Luke 5:18-25; 6:6-10; Mark 5:2-15; 9:14-27; Matt. 11:4-5; Col. 1:13; 2:13-15.

"something wrong" with man, that man is in bondage and in need of freedom. The unique aspect of the Christian perspective, however, is its own definition of what is "wrong" with man and its own measure of the extent or depth of his problem. In the New Testament, man is seen in the light of the free man, Jesus of Nazareth, and compared to him, men are not free; they are bound by fear and anxiety, mistrust and self-concern. The word used to describe this condition, when measured by *this* standard, is "sin." The logical structure of this teaching does not depend on the story of the "Fall," or even on a theory of "inherited guilt." The various traditional forms of the doctrine of "original sin" are not empirical observations about man; they are *comparative* statements of man's condition, measured by the historical standard of Jesus of Nazareth.

Christian doctrine says that sin places man under the judgment of God, the final judge being Christ. This is a development of the idea of man's measurement by the norm of Jesus. To use a norm is to compare and to judge. The connection of language about judgment with language about sin is a logical consequence of the way in which man is seen in the Christian perspective.

The radical language with which the New Testament authors speak of sin ("as in Adam all die, even so in Christ shall all be made alive")[8] becomes meaningful if it is taken as reflecting the way in which a liberated man looks back upon his "slavery." The language about sin is for the Christian a language concerning a problem answered.[9] Orthodox theology does not say that the Christian does not sin, but it sees sin as a problem to which a solution has been given. The Creeds speak of sin in this way: "I believe in . . . the forgiveness of sins." It is the language of faith and would make no sense in the mouth of one who was not a Christian. The unbeliever may speak of human

[8] I Cor. 15:22.
[9] Barth, *KD*, IV/1, § 60, I.

fear, anxiety, and bondage, but since these conditions are measured against some other norm than Jesus of Nazareth, and since
he does not speak of this problem as one who has been liberated
by the contagion of Jesus' freedom, he will speak in another
way. The word "sin" is peculiar to the historical perspective of
Christian faith and it will not retain its biblical meaning apart
from this context.[10] Christians are undoubtedly themselves responsible for making themselves incomprehensible to others and
to themselves by speaking too much about sin and forgetting too
often the context in which the word is logically placed.

The Pelagian teaching that man sins solely by his own
choice, and not at all because of the condition into which he is
born, is incompatible with the Christian perspective, not so
much because it is an inadequate description of the human
problem, as because it reflects an inadequate appreciation of
Easter. It is true that Pelagianism has a naïve conception of
human freedom. More basic than this, however, is its failure to
take adequate account of the fact that in the historical perspective of the Christian, freedom has come as a result of Easter and
the Gospel of Easter. On the other hand, traditional theology
has rejected the extreme alternative: that sin is "natural" to
man. Such a teaching would indicate that one had taken one's
definition of man from man in bondage ("Adam"), and not
from the free man Jesus of Nazareth.

JUSTIFICATION What the Gospel finally has to say
about sin is that it has been dealt with on the cross once for all,
that man has received justification by sheer grace in the event of
Easter, and that this gift is to be received and acknowledged in
faith. The doctrine of justification by grace through faith expresses the believer's conviction that he has been accepted freely,
regardless of his merit, because of Christ. If it is understood
empirically, it puts us in a cosmological courtroom which is

[10] John 15:22.

logically meaningless and morally doubtful.[11] Understood as the expression of the believer's historical perspective, however, it indicates that his freedom is such that he no longer feels the need to "prove" himself to himself or to anyone else. He is free to accept himself, convinced that he is acceptable, for he has been set free by Jesus of Nazareth. His acceptance is simply his trust in the declaration, "Neither do I condemn you,"[12] and he acknowledges this word and its speaker, not his own history, as the basis of his perspective. Bultmann has spoken in existential terms of the new self-understanding of the believer. Set in the context of a historical perspective, wider than a merely personal one, Bultmann's interpretation of justification would be in order. The existentialist interpretation is liable to misunderstanding, however, precisely in its emphasis on *self*-understanding, which might lead to a doctrine of justification by means of faith, rather than grace. Such a misunderstanding will be avoided by emphasizing the discernment situation occasioned by the Gospel; what is newly understood is not first of all the self, but Jesus of Nazareth. This way of speaking is logically parallel to the assertion of the apostle that Jesus was raised from the dead for "our" justification.[13] After that has been said, it is then in order to speak of a new self-understanding, which is a significant part of a new "blik."

SANCTIFICATION The declaration "Neither do I condemn you" is followed by the command "Go and do not sin again."[14] The inseparable connection and the clear distinction between justification and sanctification have received their classic definition in the analysis of Calvin.[15] According to Calvin,

[11] For an attempt to remove the moral ambiguity (but not the logical meaninglessness!) in the classical Protestant doctrine of justification, cf. van Buren, *op. cit.,* pp. 73 ff., 118 ff.
[12] John 8:11.
[13] Rom. 4:25.
[14] John 8:11.
[15] *Institutes,* III, i, 1; xi, 1 *et passim;* cf. xiv and xviii.

both are the result of incorporation into Christ by the Holy Spirit. Being united with Christ, the believer shares in both his righteousness and his holiness. He is set free and at the same time he is set on a specific road. One action is completed, final, unqualified. He is a free man. The other is a movement, a pressing forward, a task in which he lives. Considered once more as language expressing the Christian's perspective, the doctrine of sanctification clarifies the nature of his freedom: like the freedom of Jesus himself, it is freedom to be concerned and compassionate, to become involved for the sake of our neighbor in the world about us. As Luther said of the Christian, he is free to become a slave of his neighbor.[16] The relationship between completed justification and the march along the road of sanctification can also be expressed as the relationship between faith and love. Faith is the thankful acknowledgment of liberation and one's liberator. Love is the fruit of this, the exercise of this freedom in serving one's neighbor. In a word, sanctification is love for one's neighbor.

It might be objected that this interpretation ignores the double command of love with which Jesus summarized the Law. Did he not say that love for God was the first commandment and that love for the neighbor was second?[17] Bornkamm's discussion of this in his *Jesus von Nazareth*[18] reveals the problem behind this question. He insists that "in Jesus' preaching, love toward God invariably has priority," yet much the larger part of Bornkamm's interpretation of the double command is devoted to love for the neighbor. He asks, "Are love toward God and love toward the neighbor one and the same?" and answers, "Certainly not. . . . Whoever equates in this fashion the two commandments knows nothing of God's sovereignty and will very soon turn God into a mere word or symbol with which one might as well dis-

---

[16] *Von der Freiheit eines Christenmenschen,* in *Werke in Auswahl,* O. Clemens, ed. (Berlin: Walter de Grunter & Co., 1950), Vol. II, pp. 11 ff.

[17] Matt. 22:37-39.

[18] G. Bornkamm, *Jesus von Nazareth* (Stuttgart: Kohlhammer, 1956), pp. 101 ff. (109 ff.).

pense." (In passing, we might say that this is closing the barn door several centuries too late.) Bornkamm continues: "Surrender to God means . . . being awake and ready for God, *who claims me in other men*. In this sense, love for the neighbor is the test of love for God."[19] Precisely. If love for the neighbor is the test of "love for God," then by the verification principle it is the meaning of "love for God."[20] What is "being ready for God" other than being ready for the neighbor? Is it not significant that we, and apparently Bornkamm also, cannot find other words for it? But if the Logos, which is God, has really been made flesh, as orthodox theology has maintained, then we have no need to speak about anything other than this "flesh" which dwelt among us. The command to love God first and the command to love the neighbor, when taken together, can only mean that we are to love the neighbor on the model of Jesus and in his freedom. He has set the believer free for the service of the good Samaritan, who came to the man lying by the roadside simply because he was a man in need, and who offered help where it was needed. In hearing this parable, the Christian recognizes that he himself is the man left by the roadside who has been rescued. He recognizes that the key to the parable is the man who first told it, and in the freedom for which he has been set free, he is able to hear the concluding, "Go and do thou likewise," as words of command which point him on his way, the way of love leading toward the neighbor.

The Church, Its Acts and Words

The Christian does not hold his historical perspective alone, but in company with others. He comes to this perspective, moreover, because other men have had it before him. In biblical language, in becoming a Christian, he becomes a member of the

---

[19] *Ibid.*, pp. 101, 102. (110, 111); italics mine.
[20] This is just the point of I John 4:20, "If any one says 'I love God,' and hates his brother, he is a liar."

church. The difficulty is that we do not speak biblical language. In ordinary use, including the use of Christians when they are not rather self-consciously doing theology, the word "church" refers to a building: we go to church; the church is at such and such an address; it cost so many dollars to build. The linguistic difficulty arising from the difference between the biblical and ordinary uses of the word is nothing, however, compared to the theological problem of holding together biblical assertions concerning the *ekklesia* and descriptions of the sociological unit to which the biblical statements are supposed to apply. What appears sociologically to be an odd sort of club is often spoken of theologically as the "body of Christ." This is obviously not a description. It is a reference to the historical perspective which the members presumably have in common, and it suggests the harmony that would exist between people who shared this perspective.

A man becomes a Christian in the context of this community of believers, directly or indirectly. Conversion has not always come from hearing the Gospel spoken. It has also arisen from simply being with men set free "in Christ," so that the freedom of Jesus has been contagious through Christians. Athanasius, in his essay on the Incarnation, offers as "proof" of the resurrection of Jesus and of his living power as Lord precisely the freedom of Christians, their liberation from the bondage of superstition and wasted lives, their freedom to love even their enemies and to face death unafraid as Jesus' disciples.[21] Because Athanasius did not see these signs as evidence of the power or superiority of the church or of the Christian religion, he could attribute the "success" of the Christian mission to the contagious freedom of Jesus. The "church" was the people who shared in this freedom and were aware of its source. Held together by a shared perspective based on the history of the free man who had set them free, they were, logically, the "community of the resurrection."

[21] *De incarn.,* chap. 20.

B A P T I S M   Christians have from the earliest times preserved a peculiar act of initiation into their historical perspective: the rite of baptism. Baptism is traditionally performed in the midst of the congregation, for it concerns not only the candidate, but also those who have already been baptized. In its original form, baptism was a dramatic representation of what happens when one changes "bliks": the candidate was immersed in water, "buried," or "washed clean" (according to various New Testament passages), and raised up as a person with a new life given to him, a "new man." This rite represented the dramatic change which Christians felt lay between their past bondage and their present liberty, between the world as it had appeared before and the world as it was seen with their new perspective. Baptism dramatizes this difference not only for the one who is baptized, but also for those who witness this act.

P R E A C H I N G   One of the traditional "marks" of the "true church" is preaching. One member of the congregation stands before the others and speaks. In the Protestant tradition (and to some extent in Catholicism as well), this speaking has a peculiar relationship to the Bible. Passages of the Bible are read aloud. A particular passage is singled out as a "text," on the basis of which a "sermon" is preached. The sermon is primarily a proclamation, for it points to the free man of Nazareth as the story of Easter does; the sermon presents him as the source and the norm of the Christian's perspective and freedom. A sermon may therefore be an occasion for the renewal and deepening of the hearer's historical perspective. And if he has not previously been a Christian, it may become the occasion of a discernment that leads him to hold this perspective. This is the meaning of the traditional assertion that preaching which is faithful to the biblical witness to the "Word of God" may become itself the "Word of God."[22]

---

[22] For example, the wording of the prayers having to do with preaching in the American *The Book of Common Prayer* (1928), pp. 244, 547, 566.

Preaching has the further function of illustrating the perspective of Christian faith. The preacher points to the present situation of the world and suggests how some aspect of this world looks to "eyes of faith."[23] The hearer is invited to stretch his imagination, to extend the range of his historical perspective, in order that he may see the world in which he lives in the light of Jesus of Nazareth as the liberator of the whole world, not just of believers. He is told that he may and that he can, rather than that he should, see the world in this way. The "blik" which is illustrated and commended in preaching will always be related explicity or implicitly to its historical basis, however. The sermon is said to be based on a text from the Bible, and this appeal to the documents which recount the history of Jesus, the people from which he came and of which he was a part, and the disciples who came to share in his freedom, reflects the historical aspect of the Christian perspective.

Preaching may also take the secondary form of exhortation. It will be recalled that Anthony Flew objects that if "you ought because it is God's will" means no more than "you ought," it is either silly or dishonest.[24] Our answer to this objection is that Flew has misunderstood the function of exhortation in preaching. The clause "because it is God's will" points to the context of the exhortation, to the history of Jesus and of Easter and the invitation to see the world in the light of that history. The hearer is invited to see a particular problem in a manner consistent with this perspective. The sermon suggests that if he does in fact have this perspective, he "ought" *logically* to see the problem in a certain way, and this would lead *logically* to certain acts. The "because it is God's will" is not an explanation of why a Christian ought to act in a certain way; it points to the historical perspective which provides a context for such an action. In this context, the statement is neither silly nor dishonest, but intelligible and meaningful. It may be granted, however, that "because

---

[23] Cf. P. Minear, *Eyes of Faith* (London: Lutterworth, 1948).
[24] *New Essays*, p. 108.

it is God's will" appears to be an explanation and that other words might have been chosen to indicate more clearly that reference is being made to a historical perspective.

THE LORD'S SUPPER When Christians gather for their weekly celebration of Easter, there takes place the "preaching of the Word" and also the celebration of the Lord's Supper, a memorial of the last meal Jesus had with his disciples. The logic of this memorial is revealed in one of the stories of the Easter appearances of Jesus to his disciples, which is set in the context of a meal: in the breaking of bread, "the light dawned" and Jesus was seen in a new way.[25] Similarly, the Lord's Supper is celebrated to provide an opportunity for the believer to "see" more clearly the basis of his "blik" and be "renewed" in his faith. The invitation to "feed" on Jesus himself in the sixth chapter of the Gospel of John is a blunt way of saying that faith has to do with the "flesh" of Jesus, with Jesus as a concrete historical man.[26] This odd language underscores the essential role of this history in the Christian perspective, a role dramatized in the celebration of the Lord's Supper.

The language traditionally associated with this symbolic meal has led to debates concerning "the real presence" of Christ. Some have held that he is present in the bread and wine itself, others that he is present in a more general way, as host of this supper. Still others have maintained that the meal is only an act of commemoration. These differences cannot be settled empirically. The language of Catholic theology, by insisting that the physical properties of the bread and wine remain unchanged in spite of their "substantial" transformation into the body and blood of Christ, excludes an empirical verification of this "presence." The assertion of a "real presence" is, again, the peculiar language of a discernment situation. It is related to the language of Easter: the apostles' assertion that Jesus appeared to them,

[25] Luke 24:28-31.
[26] John 6:52-59.

and the later tradition of bodily appearances. When the believer receives the bread with the words, "This is my body which is given for you," and if this becomes for him a discernment situation, he will say that he suddenly "saw" that Jesus' freedom was for him. He might even say that it was as if Jesus were there before him offering himself. The assertion of a "real presence," therefore, means that the celebration of the Lord's Supper has and may again become a discernment situation, and that the believer's liberation is as genuine as that of the disciples, being ultimately derived from Jesus himself by way of Easter.

PRAYER   No outline of the theological consequences of our interpretation would be complete without dealing with prayer. Surely, it will be objected, prayer cannot be simply an aspect of a historical perspective, for it is addressed to someone. However difficult the problem of speaking *about* God may be, surely we must understand faith so as to account for speaking *to* God. Admittedly, the language of prayer is the language of address, of speaking to someone, but the empirical attitude of our secular thinking leaves us puzzled if we are asked to posit "someone" to whom to speak in prayer. We must look in another direction if we would find a secular meaning of prayer.

When ancient man prayed that God send rain on his neighbor's fields, he thought he was doing the most effective thing he could in the exercise of his perspective as a Christian. Called to freedom for his neighbor, he set out to help him. The best help he knew was God, and his neighbor needed rain, so that to help was to pray for rain. That was the use and the meaning of his prayer. In a similar situation today, a Christian's actions will differ, although he will be doing the same thing: he will reflect on his neighbor's plight in the light of the Gospel. He will begin by trying to see this situation in the light of his historical perspective. He has been set free from self-concern in order to be concerned for his neighbor. He will therefore set about doing just what ancient man was doing: the most effective thing he

knows of to relieve his neighbor's distress. Assuming that he is
just as serious about this as the Christian of ancient times, who
may have prayed and fasted for days, he will go to see his neighbor, study the situation with him, and see what can be done to
get water on the fields by irrigation or other means. If no solution is possible, he will at the least stand by his neighbor and
help him through the hard times resulting from crop failure.
After all, prayer sometimes went "unanswered" in ancient times,
too. If he can give no concrete help to his neighbor, then he has
the task of seeing this situation, too, in the light of the historical
perspective of faith. "Bearing one another's burdens" will have
to take another form, in which freedom will have to show itself
as freedom to face failure. The meaning of intercessory prayer
is its use: it begins in reflection upon the situation in the light
of the Christian perspective and leads to appropriate action.

There are, of course, many situations in which we are not
able to do anything constructive. Perhaps it lies outside our
control (a problem in international relations for the "little
man" who has no influence with his national leaders), or pos-
sibly it is a situation in which even offering help might only
make matters worse (the marriage problems of a near relative).
It might be said that prayers of intercession in such cases do not
consist of anything other than simply holding the situation up
to God. But this is just what is done in what we have called "reflection." The Christian holds the situation in one hand and the
basis of his historical perspective in the other, and he tries to
submit his understanding of one to his understanding of the
other. With his newspaper in one hand, to put it figuratively,
and his Bible in the other, he tries to read the first in the light
of the second, and perhaps he will also find the second opening
his eyes to new aspects of the former. In fact, he will be doing
what a preacher does in preparing a sermon. He may conclude
that he has nothing to say or do, but he will have at least exercised himself in the intensity of thought which the Christian
"blik" demands.

Thanksgiving may be understood as the expression of the joy of a man who has found a measure of freedom and who sees signs of this freedom in the world about him. Thanksgiving and adoration express his joy and wonder before the fact that the world is and that he is, and that his historical perspective gives him a way of understanding both himself and the world.

The reason why prayer is difficult for many men today is that its traditional language leads them to imagine something which contradicts their empirical attitudes. No wonder prayer seems to be a flight from "reality." It was not so for ancient man, however, and if the logic of prayer—its function in the context of the Christian's historical perspective—is understood, it need not be so today. Prayer understood as reflection and consequent action may be time-consuming and hard, but it is a perfectly conceivable and logically clear activity.

THE CHURCH'S MISSION It may be noticed that we have not even mentioned the mission of the church. We have said nothing about "preaching the Gospel to the heathen" or "bringing the world to Christ." A historical observation is in order here. In all his letters to his various readers, the apostle Paul never urged them to go out and convert unbelievers. The slogan, "each one bring one," has its roots in the nineteenth century, not in the first. The mission proclaimed in the New Testament is the mission of God to the world in Jesus Christ; the church believed that its "mission" consisted in co-operating with this "divine mission." In the name of God's mission, the church claimed the world for Christ, and as the centuries passed, the known world and the church became coextensive. But then, during the medieval period, this coextension led to a confusion which was exemplified in the rise of the power of the papacy over that of the emperor. The world came to be claimed for the church rather than for Christ.

Another consequence of this coextension was that the church had to find a new way to understand the New Testament distinction between the church and the world. This was found in the distinction between the sacred and the secular, between the "this-worldly" and the "otherworldly." The biblical "God in history" came to be understood as a "God above history." As "this world" came to be understood more and more in human terms, "God" became more and more "otherworldly," and today we no longer know how to use the word at all.

If the history of the dissolution of the claim of the church over the world and the significance of the sacred is seen in the light of the Christian perspective, the Renaissance and modern history may represent a movement of liberation.[27] If man is slowly learning to stand on his own feet and to help his neighbor without reference to the "God hypothesis," the Christian should rejoice, even if he may not overlook the danger of pride in this new freedom compared to the humble freedom of Jesus of Nazareth. The contemporary meaning of "claiming the world for Christ" cannot be a return to medieval metaphysics and the confusion of the power of the church with the contagious power of the freedom of Jesus. The meaning of that claim now is simply that the whole world may be seen with the Christian's perspective. He need not ask nor expect the world to understand itself as he understands it. Since he has acquired this perspective in connection with a freedom which is contagious, he should be content to let this contagion work its own way in the world, without his taking thought for the morrow, especially the morrow of the church.

The mission of the Christian is the way of love upon which he finds himself, the way toward the neighbor, not the way of trying to make others into Christians. His mission is simply to be a man, as this is defined by Jesus of Nazareth. It is not particularly appropriate in our time, when the church has talked far too much to the world, for him to tell his neighbor why he is "for" him. It is quite enough that he practice the liberty for

[27] Cf. R. G. Smith, *The New Man* (London, SCM Press, 1956).

which he has been set free. It is for this reason that we agree when Barth says that theology is done by the church, takes place within the church, and is for the church.[28] It is also for this reason that we questioned earlier the concern with evangelism and preaching to "modern man" which informs the theology of Bultmann and Ogden.

In an era in which men are being called to patriotism, nationalism, racial superiority, and the preservation of economic systems and various ways of life, in the name of religion, "God," the church, and all that is "holy," the clarification of the language of faith and of the Gospel by means of linguistic analysis is much needed. The chief benefactor of this clarification is the empirically-minded man who has been touched by the Gospel and who seeks a meaning and a logic to being a Christian in the world today. He is "in the world" in any case, part of public life by virtue of his job and his citizenship. How he is in that world is another question. This question receives an answer from the Christian historical perspective, but this is not the place to argue on behalf of it. What we have hoped to accomplish by this analysis is the clarification of what is involved in the Christian orientation, whether one accepts or rejects that answer. The issue of faith can be at least made comprehensible by logical analysis.

[28] Barth, *KD*, I/1, § 1.

IX

CONCLUSION:

SECULAR CHRISTIANITY

A CHRISTIAN who is himself a secular man may understand the Gospel in a secular way by seeing it as an expression of a historical perspective. That statement constitutes a recommendation to understand secularism in a particular way. Our study describes a path which may be followed by one who holds certain empirical attitudes which we feel may be widely shared by Christians in the West today. We have neither urged that this path be taken nor denied that there are alternatives. A Christian who does not share or will not acknowledge that he shares these attitudes will hardly find our path attractive. He may feel that the kind of empirical grounding which we have disclosed for the language of faith is inadequate or even inappropriate for faith. If we were to call his a more "religious" position than ours, then we might call the way which we have traveled the path of secular Christianity.

When we say that contemporary thought is secular, we are calling attention to certain characteristics of the way we think and speak today. We have not argued that ours is a better or worse mode of thought than that of ancient times. In this sense, we mean to be descriptive, not doctrinaire, when we call contemporary thinking secular. In England in the middle of the last century, secularism was a new idea, often proclaimed enthusiastically as the solution to the problem of human error and ignorance. It was attacked by the defenders of orthodoxy and tradition as atheism, but that was a misnomer: in the minds of George Jacob Holyoake and the British secularists, it was merely an agnosticism about "otherworldly" powers and beings. For the true secularist, atheism was, as much as theism, a presumptuous doctrine without foundations.[1] Today, however, we are not inclined to share the enthusiasm of the nineteenth-century secularists in their debates with entrenched traditionalists. The traditionalists are less well-entrenched; secularism, in one form or another, has become too universal a feature of our times to generate such heat. More important, however, is the fact that we are less sure about the character of secularism. Are we really being descriptive when we call the world secular? If so, it is a most imprecise description. As we are using the word, concern for men, convictions that life is worth living in a certain way, and a high valuation on human relationships are compatible with secular thought. On the other hand, when a Soviet astronaut says that he did not find God in outer space, his remark is dismissed as silly, as a reflection of an element in Soviet ideology which strikes us in the West as simply anachronistic. Our empirical attitudes are such that we are prepared to dismiss that remark in a way in which we would not care to dismiss the statement that men are only machines. It is worth noting that Holyoake would have reacted in the same way. If we conclude that we are secular in some way similar to the British secularists

---

[1] Cf. G. J. Holyoake, *The Origin and Nature of Secularism* (London: Watts, 1896). In the face of ecclesiastical opposition in England in 1853 and following years, Holyoake led a movement proclaiming a "new" agnostic humanism which he called "secularism." His intention was clearly to acknowledge the modern world, not to teach some new doctrine, but Holyoake's secularism was surely loaded with commitments, both humanist and empirical. It was as much a doctrine as the position of his ecclesiastical opponents was a doctrine.

of the last century, then we must admit that we too are not being simply descriptive when we call the world and ourselves "secular." We are saying that it is possible today to be agnostic about "otherworldly" powers and beings, but that people matter, that we live in a world in which "I" is not "you" and neither is completely assimilable to "it" or even to "he." We are urging that Buber's distinction matters more than distinctions between eternity and time, infinity and finite, and many other distinctions that mattered to Christians in another age. It is this difference between us and our ancestors to which we wish to call attention when we speak of secular Christianity.

When we affirm a secular Christianity, we also call attention to the "this-worldly" aspect of the Gospel. We have done this by exploring the empirical footing of the language of the Gospel and Christian faith, its function as it is used by men to express and communicate their understanding of the world in an age in which statements about "how things are" are expected to have some sort of relationship to men's experience of each other and of things. It may be seen, therefore, that as our understanding of secularism has influenced our understanding of the Gospel, so our understanding of the Gospel has influenced our use of the word secular.

We have made use of the method of certain linguistic analysts because their method reflects the empirical attitudes which appear to us characteristic of secular thought. It is a method which allows us to say what we want, but it also reminds us that we may ignore the logic of language only at the price of confusion. It points out that once we have seen this logic, we shall find that there are some things which we shall not want to say. We have tried to follow this method consistently without resorting to a use of words of which we can give no logical account.

Linguistic analysis exposes the function of language in just those areas on which modern theology seeks to shed light: the world in which the "average" Christian finds himself. Theologians concerned with the "relevance" of the Gospel for ordinary believers in their ordinary life and ordinary work should be particularly open to a method of analysis which appeals so frequently to the ordinary use of language. Its functional definition of meaning is consistent with the functionalism of a technological age. By means of a functional analysis of language, it shows the various empirical footings of different theological assertions, and it suggests ways in which the meaning of apparently transempirical aspects of the language of Christian faith may be understood. In this way, linguistic analysis is a valuable tool for determining the secular meaning of the Gospel.

Our study is a work of translation in the broadest sense, but in throwing light on certain major questions, it goes beyond the work of translation, for it involves a decision about the location of the center of theology. When we discussed Ogden's question about the heart of the Gospel—whether it lies in the area of Theology or in that of Christology—we said that if the question were put that way, we should be obliged to choose Christology as the center from which to understand the Gospel in a secular way. This choice has been confirmed by our investigation.

When the language of the Gospel is analyzed so as to reveal its logical meaning or function, the history of Jesus of Nazareth proves to be indispensable to it; if this history is pushed into the background, faith may be a perspective, but it is either not historical at all, or it is grounded in some other piece of history. Protestantism has known and continues to know both of these alternatives. One does not have to look far to see versions of Christianity which are either quite unrelated to history and matters of this world, "religion" becoming a "private" affair, or which are based on national history and a sense of national identity. The widespread confusion in American Protestantism (which is documented by the studies of sociologists)[2] of the so-called "American Way of Life" with the Christian faith is a clear sign of this. The assumption of many Western Christians that they should be anti-Communists for the reason that com-

---

[2] Cf. W. Herberg, *Protestant—Catholic—Jew* (Garden City, N. Y.: Doubleday, 1955).

munism is officially atheistic reflects a perspective which is in danger of losing touch with the history of Jesus of Nazareth. The real issue appears to be one of national, political, and economic commitments, but the bearing of the historical perspective of faith upon this question is lost in a concentration of attention on the meaningless issue of atheism. One way to describe the crisis of Protestantism in our time is to say that private life and national identity have combined to displace the history of Jesus and Easter as the determining ground of the Christian perspective.

On the other hand, there would have been no Gospel but for Easter. Classical Christology placed the primary emphasis on the divine rather than the human "nature" of Christ. We have seen that this means that the Christian has not simply decided to commit himself to the history of Jesus, but he has been grasped by that history in spite of himself. A "Jesusology," an attempt to begin and end with the historical Jesus as the basis of faith, not only ignores the historical finding that Jesus refused to claim anything for himself, but, more important, it involves dropping Easter out of the Gospel. The result would not be the secular meaning of the Gospel, therefore, for the Gospel is the Easter proclamation concerning Jesus of Nazareth. Granting that Jesus is indispensable to the Gospel, it must also be said that the history of Jesus without Easter is no basis for Christian faith. When Easter is in the center of the picture, however, we can then say that the meaning of the Gospel is to be found in the areas of the historical and the ethical, not in the metaphysical or the religious.

The decision to interpret the Gospel as a secular Christology, however, raises an obvious question: Although traditional theology does have a historical, intentional, and ethical dimension, does it not include a good deal more? Where, as one reviewer asked of Professor Ramsey, is the transcendent God of classical Christianity?[3] Have we not reduced theology to ethics? Our

---

[3] H. D. Lewis, "Freedom and Immortality," *The Hibbert Journal*, Vol. LIX, No. 2 (January, 1961), 173.

answer takes the form of another question: In a secular age, what would that "more" be? It is our inability to find any empirical linguistic anchorage for that "more" that has led to our interpretation. If this is a reduction in the content of theology, it is the sort of reduction which has been made by modern culture in many fields. Astrology has been "reduced" to astronomy, for example; we have excluded from the study of the stars a cosmological or metaphysical theory about their effect on human life. Alchemy was "reduced" to chemistry by the rigorous application of an empirical method. During the Renaissance, the metaphysical ideas and purposes of medieval painting were excluded, leaving "only" the work of art. In almost every field of human learning, the metaphysical and cosmological aspect has disappeared and the subject matter has been "limited" to the human, the historical, the empirical. Theology cannot escape this tendency if it is to be a serious mode of contemporary thought, and such a "reduction" of content need no more be regretted in theology than in astronomy, chemistry, or painting. To speak in traditional terms again, has not orthodox theology said that God has set his heart on man, that he has come to meet and love man in the only way men can know or speak of love, namely as a man and on the human level? Does not such a God thereby reveal that he wants men to stop trying to peer into the clouds and to obey God's will by thinking out their existence in terms of man—specifically the man in whom God has said all that he has to say to men?

It may be objected that we have spent all our time speaking of the freedom of man, whereas the apostle Paul was concerned primarily for the glory of God. What exactly is the difference? What is the meaning of being concerned for the "glory of God," and how can one who has this concern be identified? According to Paul himself, whatever light is to be thrown on the knowledge of the "glory of God" is to be found in the face of Christ.[4] We would agree that the "glory of God" may be spoken of only

[4] II Cor. 4:6.

in terms of that man. Being concerned for that "glory" means being concerned for that man. The fact that the language of our interpretation of Jesus and Easter is different from that of Paul does not preclude the possibility that our meaning and Paul's may be the same.

Our results were reached by considering the language of the Gospel in relation to the language of certain kinds of human experience. If no family resemblances were allowed between the language of the Gospel and the way in which we speak of being loved by another human being, we should have to abandon all hope of understanding what the Gospel means. But languages do have family resemblances, and it is by noticing them as well as by seeing their limits that we can understand the language of theology. The verification principle shows that theological statements which are meaningless in a secular age when they are taken as straightforward empirical assertions about the world, nevertheless prove to have a use and a meaning as the expressions of a historical perspective with far-reaching empirical consequences in a man's life. In the last analysis, a tree is known by its fruit. While much may still be unknown about the dynamics of freedom and of the effect of a liberated man upon other men, enough is known of this effect to indicate what the Christian means when he says that he sees all of life in the light of the Easter proclamation concerning Jesus.

A further asset of our method is that it has produced a secular interpretation of Christianity which is not sectarian. The analysis of the language of classical Christology and of some of the major doctrines of Christian faith connects our interpretation with the long history of Christian theology. It is a temptation in a secular age to discard that tradition as so much meaningless metaphysics, but to do so jeopardizes the possibility of a fair interpretation of the full Gospel. The path which we have described for the secular Christian in the secular world is clear and wide enough to carry the whole Gospel along it. Although we have admitted that our interpretation represents a reduction of Christian faith to its historical and ethical dimensions, we would also claim that we have left nothing essential behind. This claim stands or falls with our interpretation of the language connected with Easter.

We would remind the believer who shares Flew's opinion— that faith interpreted simply as a "blik" is not Christian at all —that from Peter's confrontation with Cornelius and the debate concerning the entry of the Gentiles into the all-Jewish early church, down through the history of Christian thought and life, there has been more than one way of expressing the substance of the Gospel. We might also observe that Christians were once called atheists by a misunderstanding, but religious, culture. If there are some who feel that our interpretation is too radical, they should remember that only certain alternatives are available in our time. The other choices are even less attractive, whether they are a sectarian secularism which ignores essential elements of the Gospel, giving us a faith without Christ or a Christ without Jesus, or a very orthodox but meaningless faith which refuses to enter the secular world. The way which we have followed is admittedly conditioned by the particular attitudes with which we began this investigation, but it has led us to an interpretation which may claim for a secular Christianity the full tradition of the faith.[5]

---

[5] The plea implied in this last paragraph is ably and more fully developed by J. A. T. Robinson in his *Honest to God* (London: SCM Press, 1963), which I have been privileged to read in proof. It is to be hoped that the spirit of open and honest exploration there advocated may prevail in theology in the period into which we are now moving, a period in which Christians have to discover the secular meaning of the Gospel. Bishop Robinson agrees with me that this discovery depends upon a radical reconsideration of theological method. The difference between our suggestions for a solution to the common problem arises out of our differing methods. Mine has been characterized by taking Christology as a starting point, rather than Theology, and by using the tool of linguistic analysis. Had Bishop Robinson reversed the order of his chapters on "The Ground of Being" and "The Man for Others," and reflected more on the language involved in both areas, our conclusions would have been even more similar than they are.

NAME INDEX

SUBJECT INDEX

203